How to BUILD a BILLY CART and ➔ OTHER FUN stuff!

FOR MY FAMILY—Gwenllian and our children, Gruffydd,
Branwen and Greta, the band of positivity in every day   R.P.

Scholastic Australia
345 Pacific Highway Lindfield NSW 2070
An imprint of Scholastic Australia Pty Limited
PO Box 579 Gosford NSW 2250
ABN 11 000 614 577
www.scholastic.com.au

Part of the Scholastic Group
Sydney • Auckland • New York • Toronto • London • Mexico City
• New Delhi • Hong Kong • Buenos Aires • Puerto Rico

Published by Scholastic Australia in 2016.
Text copyright © Rob Palmer, 2016.
Illustrations and additional text © Scholastic Australia, 2016. Illustrations and additional text by Matt Francis.
Photography © Scholastic Australia, 2016. Photographs by Ryan Kitching.
Additional illustrations: Tools background © Tribalium | Shutterstock.com;
Closeup of ball and football goal © Jan_S | Shutterstock.com

National Library of Australia Cataloguing-in-Publication entry
Creator: Palmer, Rob, author.
Title: How to build a billy cart and other fun stuff / Rob Palmer.
ISBN: 9781743625743 (hardback)
Target Audience: For primary school age.
Subjects: Coaster cars--Design and construction--Juvenile literature.
        Creative activities and seat work--Juvenile literature.
Dewey Number: 371.3

Typeset in Din, ClickClack, Oleo and Oswald.

Printed in China by RR Donnelley.
Scholastic Australia's policy, in association with RR Donnelley, is to use papers that are renewable and are
made efficiently from wood grown in responsibly managed forests, so as to minimise its environmental
footprint.

10 9 8 7 6 5 4 3 2 1   16 17 18 19 20 / 1

How to BUILD a BILLY CART and → OTHER FUN Stuff!

16 FUN DIY PROJECTS to make together!

ROB PALMER

Drawings and additional text by Matt Francis

A Scholastic Australia Book

G'DAY

and welcome to a collection of my most favourite and achievable DIY projects. They range from the ridiculously simple to the slightly more complicated.

To get to the point, this book is all about fun. The projects have been chosen with families in mind, working together, taking the opportunity to have some old-school fun and mechanical play.

Just for some background—I was very lucky as a kid. I had unconditional love from my parents (great start!), and Dad loved to make stuff. Dad didn't have a guide book or a reference other than his knowledge of building which, to pump Dad up a bit, is really awesome. We enjoyed a homemade swing set, a cubby house in a tree, DIY fibreglassed water slide and heaps more.

Dad inspired me to have a crack at things with my mates, too. Some worked (those jumps for pushbikes were great!), some weren't so clever.

There was the gradual twisting and steepening of a 3-ply ramp to enable a four-wheel billy cart to be driven on two wheels, just like stunt vehicles in the movies. There were a few chunks of skin lost to the road chasing that dream, but that's life!

And I won't ever forget covering half the swimming pool with a dance floor for my 18th birthday party. Talk about a brilliant move, until my mate, Ed, went in, wearing his older brother's suede leather jacket. The jacket was ruined and Ed wasn't too pleased—his brother even less so. Though it was remarkable that out of 50-odd people on the deck, only one went in the pool!

The point is, with some imagination and a little bit of know-how, there's nothing that you can't have a crack at. If you follow some sound tips and techniques, all of a sudden that toy garage that may have turned out OK will become a brilliant piece of fun that won't just fill you with pride, it'll be a piece that you'll treasure. Best of all, seeing the joy your family gets from the finished product increases your delight and pride even more.

The great thing is that it's not just dads and mums who can DIY; when you make something with your kids, the whole project becomes an adventure of practical learning and family fun. So take my advice—start simple, and as you gain confidence, you're near to a deadset certainty of creating awesome projects you'll amaze yourself with, and will probably even encourage your mates to jump on the DIY bandwagon! So remember: **D**are. **I**magine. **Y**es, we're on our way!

CONTENTS

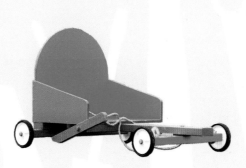

HOW TO USE THIS BOOK

DIY SKILLS

All the projects in this book have been written and illustrated with the DIY novice in mind, so any project can be tackled with very little previous DIY experience.

The projects have been given a difficulty rating, shown at the start of each section. These ratings indicate the skill level, and range from the ridiculously easy, requiring no real DIY know-how and very little time: ⚙☆☆, to the more complicated constructions that you might want to work up to: ⚙⚙⚙.

MEASUREMENTS

All measurements used throughout this book are in millimetres (mm), unless otherwise stated.

The measurements are listed showing WIDTH x THICKNESS x LENGTH, unless otherwise stated. For sheet materials, like plywood, the measurements are listed showing LENGTH x WIDTH x THICKNESS.

Ø indicates the diameter size, in mm, of round materials, like dowel and tubing.

MATERIALS

I've included Shopping Lists for each project so it's super easy to make sure you have all the materials you need before you begin a project. There's nothing worse than starting a project and realising part-way through that you don't have enough dowel or timber to finish it off. Take a photo of the Shopping List on your phone so you can check it when you go to the store.

All of the materials I've suggested to use should be readily available at your hardware store. These recommendations are what I have used to build these projects. You can substitute other materials, and use what you have around your shed—just don't forget to make adjustments to the project for those materials, and don't expect it to look exactly like the pictures of what I've made!

Remember! The items listed in the Shopping Lists show the amounts that are required to build each particular project. These measurements won't always be exactly the same size as what's available to buy in store. (For example, if the Shopping List says you'll need an 800mm length of dowel, you may need to purchase the next closest length available—900mm or 1200mm). Many of these projects use similar materials and hardware though, so any extras can be saved and used in your next DIY project!

TOOL BOXES

See page 8 for a list of all the basic tools that are good to have in your tool box. I like to keep a variety of extra consumables like drill bits, sandpaper, glue and pencils on hand—you'll always need them, and it's a pain when you run out mid-build.

There are also individual Tool Box Lists at the start of each project which will show all the tools you'll need to make each job as easy and quick as possible.

SAFETY TIPS

Some of the projects have safety tips included, signalling important safety information about the construction or ongoing use of projects. Be sure to read these tips, especially when building with young children. (And you'll find more safety tips for before you start building on page 11.)

DIY FOR KIDS

These icons are included at certain steps in all the projects in this book. These are there to suggest good points in the construction process for young kids to get involved and help with the building too.

TIPS AND TECHNIQUES

I've put together some general tips and techniques that will come in handy again and again. You'll see key words in red through the instructions for every project—you'll find a tip about these topics in the TIPS AND TECHNIQUES section at the back of the book, on pages 123–127.

There are Top Tips included in each of the projects to provide extra information and make particular steps in the construction that bit easier.

TOOL BOX

You need the gear before the idea! So here's a list of the basic tools and equipment to stock up your shed or tool box. Most of the items are pretty essential; other tools on the list are optional but ideal to have, to make your DIY projects that little bit easier to get just right.

FOR MEASURING UP

Calculator

Carpenter's pencil

Chalk line set Helpful, but not essential. It will make marking up straight cutting lines and grid lines for big project templates much easier.

Combination square Are adjustable and have a 45 degree marking feature.

Metal ruler

Retractable tape measure

Straight edge/Spirit level Ideally, in two sizes:1200mm and mini (around 200–400mm).

FOR DRILLING

Cordless drill/driver One with a hammer feature is even better.

Drill bits See Consumables.

Rotary tool These will be very helpful on a number of DIY projects.

FOR CUTTING

Bench hook These are a piece of cake to make. At its most basic, it's just three pieces of timber stuck together, and it will help hold your project in place when hand sawing, planing or chiselling. With a bench hook, you can turn any surface into a perfect workspace—even the kitchen table! (See TIPS AND TECHNIQUES for how to make one.)

Circular saw or drop saw These are ideal, but not essential.

Hacksaw For sawing PVC pipe or metal.

Hardpoint handsaw These are the cheapest type of handsaw, and are very effective, but they cannot be resharpened.

Jigsaw A jigsaw will do for most of the projects. Have a few different types of blades, including scrolling, rough cut, fine cut and blades for cutting metal. Keep a couple of spare blades too.

Multi tool This is an oscillating tool, which means there are no spinning parts. They are usually adaptable for sanding as well, so you get a couple of tools in one. They are not designed for cutting larger sections of timber.

Scissors

Utility knife

Wire snips

CONSUMABLES

Holesaw bits In sizes 40mm and 52mm.

Nails Buy nails as you need them, though 50mm galvanised bullet heads will cover a lot of jobs. A pack of smaller panel pins will be handy too.

Screws Screw sizes are by length (usually in mm) and gauge (thickness of the shaft). They come in different types, but the most common are Phillips head and slot head. My favourite screws are 8-gauge (8g) treated pine screws with #2 Phillips head. Keep a few different lengths as they are a great all-round screw.

Set of driver bits Sets of 18 pieces or more will cover almost any job you may encounter. Buying driver bits individually can be expensive, however the quality may be better. I would also recommend keeping an extra #2 Phillips driver bit.

Set of masonry bits Ranging in sizes from 5mm to 10mm.

Set of spade/speedbor bits In sizes 12mm, 18mm, 25mm and 32mm.

Set of timber drill bits Ranging in sizes from 1mm to 10mm, plus countersink bit.

FOR STICKING

Duct tape It can do almost anything.

Hot glue gun and glue sticks Use hot glue to tack projects together when you need an instant bond.

Masking tape This may be needed when marking up or for masking up when painting.

PVA glue Use PVA for a stronger bond.

Spray adhesive

Staple gun

FOR SMOOTHING

Hand plane These aren't essential but are handy to have.

Palm/Orbital sander Plus 80, 120 and 180 grit sandpaper.

Wet and dry sandpaper Keep a supply in various grits—300, 600 and 1200—for sharpening.

FOR DECORATING

Mini rollers and tray

Paintbrushes 20mm, 50mm and 75mm are good sizes to buy. Good quality brushes well looked after will last a long time and achieve a better finish than a $2 cheapy.

FOR EVERYTHING ELSE

Adjustable wrench/shifter For tightening nuts and bolts, and will fit different sizes.

Chisels A set of 12mm, 18mm and 25mm chisels is essential.

Hammer A claw hammer is an essential item to have. A club/lump hammer is helpful to have too.

Multi grips, clamps or vices For holding small bits steady.

Pliers

Saw horses And/or a set of fold-down trestles.

Screwdrivers Slot head and Phillips head screwdrivers.

Socket spanner set

KIDS' TOOL BOX

It's great for kids to have their own set of tools too. I'd suggest starting out with the following:

Lightweight claw hammer

Paintbrushes and mini roller

Phillips head and slot head screwdrivers

Small shifting spanner

Tape measure

Tool box or tool belt

ADDITIONAL ITEMS TO USE UNDER ADULT SUPERVISION

Chisels

Handsaw

Hot glue gun

Multi tool For kids wanting to have a go at power tools, an oscillating multi tool is a good one to start with, under adult supervision. They are speed adjustable, and the blades oscillate instead of rotate, making them much safer. Best of all, they are well-suited to a wide range of tasks.

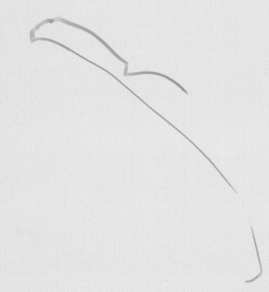

SAFETY

Safety is always the most important thing, so it's a good idea to get the right protective equipment and follow these safety tips when undertaking any project, especially when building with kids.

GEAR

Protective clothing It's best not to wear clothing that's too loose, or with pieces that could get caught in tools and equipment. If your shirt has buttons, do them up. And long sleeves aren't a bad idea either.

Safety glasses These can be bought as either glasses or goggles, and can come in kids' sizes too.

Dust masks I recommend using dust masks with Filter Class P2. These meet Australian standards and are great, all-rounder masks to use.

Gloves Have a box of disposable latex gloves on hand to use when gluing and painting.

Ear protection Ear plugs are a must when operating power tools. Kids may find earmuffs more comfortable to wear—they're easily found in junior sizes too.

Footwear Keep the sandals and thongs for the beach, and wear closed-toe shoes whenever you're DIYing just in case something drops!

SAFETY TIPS WHEN BUILDING

* Never leave children unattended around tools and equipment, and always supervise and assist children when using tools.

* Always unplug power tools when not in use.

* Remember that a battery-powered tool is as good as plugged in when the battery is attached, so remove the battery when not in use, even for short periods between tasks.

* Do not leave cords lying where you are working—they're a tripping hazard, especially for kids.

* Always clean and sand timber well to get rid of any splinters. Sand or round all corners to avoid sharp edges.

* Keep your workspace clean, and be sure to work in a well-ventilated area, especially when sanding or gluing.

HELICOPTER

Helicopters are pretty cool. Being able to put one together with an actual turning rotor blade will make you pretty cool too!

This project won't take long, and it requires very basic skills. And you can paint it up to look just like your favourite chopper.

What's more, you can use your imagination and adapt the following steps to make all kinds of different creations. Once you have drawn the profile of an object, just use the basic elements of this project and then add whatever spinning bits or wheels you need to make your idea come to life.

Another great toy I like based on this design is a duck on wheels. You can add a rope to the front and you've got a pet that waddles around the house, won't poop on the carpet and costs nothing to keep!

TOOL BOX

Clamps or vice	**Hammer**	**Palm sander** with 80 and
Drill	**Handsaw**	120 grit sandpaper
Drill bits:	**Jigsaw** (with scrolling blade)	
6mm and 10mm	**Pencil**	
32mm speedbor bit	**PVA glue**	

SHOPPING LIST

Description	Qty	Size	Material
Body	1	100 x 19 x 230	Pine
Large Dowel	1	Ø20 x 300	Pine Dowel
Small Dowel	1	Ø6 x 250	Pine Dowel
Rotors	1	30 x 8 x 220	Pine

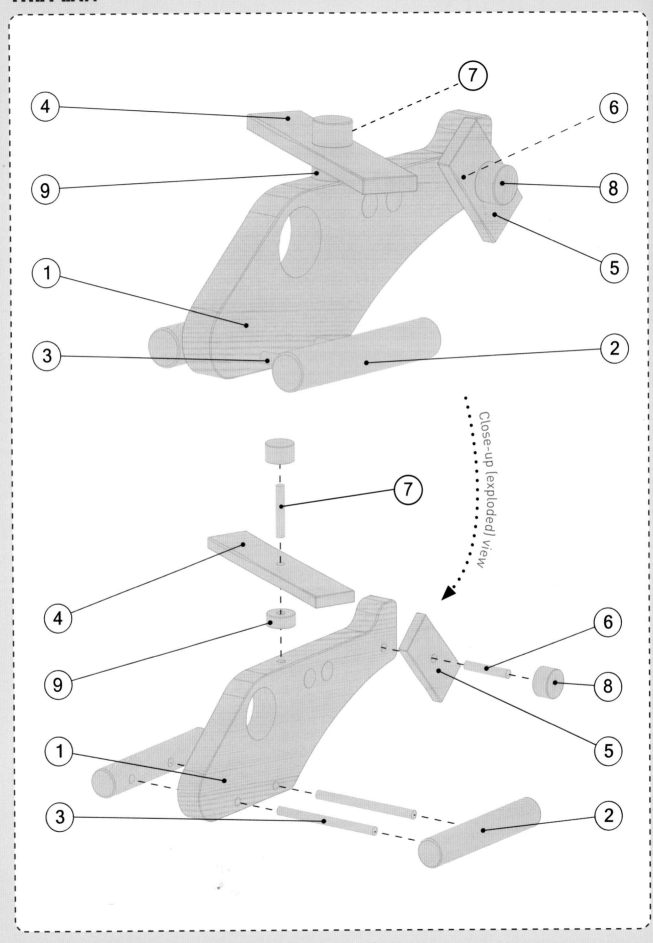

Close-up (exploded) view

THE PARTS

Part	Description	Qty	Size	Material
1	Body	1	100 x 19 x 230	Pine
2	Skid	2	Ø20 x 115	Dowel
3	Skid Brace	2	Ø6 x 80	Dowel
4	Rotor	1	30 x 8 x 155	Pine
5	Tail Rotor	1	30 x 8 x 50	Pine
6	Tail Rotor Spindle	1	Ø6 x 32	Dowel
7	Main Rotor Spindle	1	Ø6 x 50	Dowel
8	Rotor Housing	2	Ø20 x 12	Dowel
9	Rotor Spacer	1	Ø20 x 8	Dowel

INSTRUCTIONS

Step 1

Scale 1:2

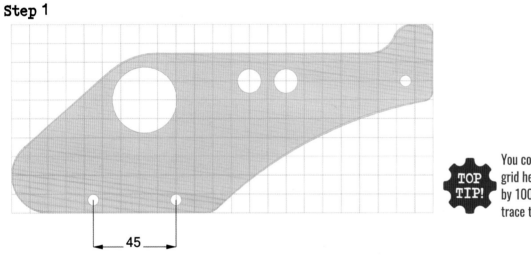

45

TOP TIP! You could photocopy the grid here and enlarge it by 100% and use it to trace the body.

a. Mark up the design of the body of the helicopter. Use a 10mm x 10mm grid as a guide.

b. Once you have drawn up the shape, drill the holes first, this makes it easier to hold the timber steady while you drill. The holes for the skid braces ③ and tail rotor spindle ⑥ are the most important to position correctly.

c. Cut the shape out with a jigsaw using a scrolling blade.

Step 2

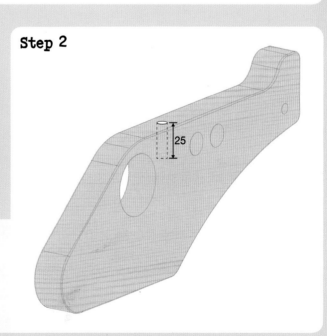

25

a. Drill the hole for the main rotor down through the top of the helicopter body, to a depth of 25mm. Use a bench vice to hold the timber steady while you drill down. (See TIPS AND TECHNIQUES for how to set up a makeshift bench vice.)

Step 3

a. Cut all the other pieces to size and sand the edges to make smooth.

 TOP TIP! If you are drilling into the centre of a small piece of timber use multi grips or a bench vice to hold the piece steady while you drill.

Step 4

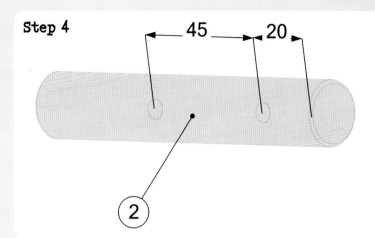

45   20

②

a. Drill two holes halfway through each skid at the distances shown.

b. Check that both holes are straight, so all the pieces will line up.

c. Make sure that the holes in the skid and the base of the helicopter body are in a position so that when the skid is connected via the braces it will sit on the ground holding the helicopter body up off the ground.

Step 5

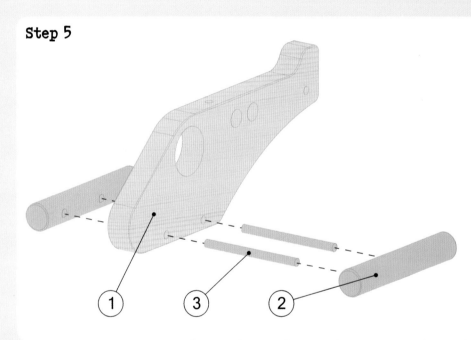

①   ③   ②

a. Attach the skids and braces, using PVA glue at any point where timber touches timber.

b. Lay the chopper body flat on your bench with the holes for the skid braces slightly hanging over the edge. This way, it is easy to hold the body as you gently tap the skid braces through with a hammer.

c. Be sure to centre the skid braces through the helicopter body, so that both skids are even on either side of the body.

Step 6

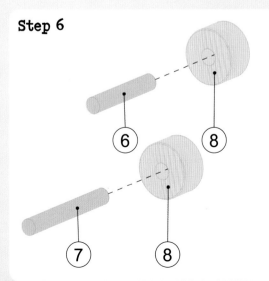

⑥   ⑧

⑦   ⑧

a. You will need to make two of these—one for the main rotor and one for the tail rotor.

b. Drill a hole in both rotor housings halfway. Check that your centring hole is the same diameter as the 6mm dowel of your spindles. (See TIPS AND TECHNIQUES for more on drilling.)

c. Glue each of the rotor spindles in the housings.

d. Wait for these to dry before fitting and attaching the rotors, to avoid getting glue on them.

Step 7

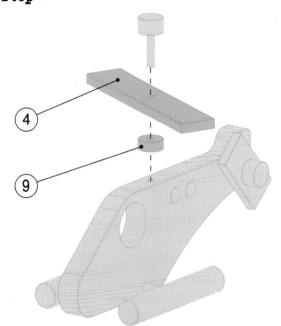

⑤

a. Drill a hole in the tail rotor, making sure that the hole is slightly larger than the dowel so it will spin freely.

b. Place a small amount of glue in the hole of the tail of the chopper body only. Slide the shorter spindle from Step 6 through the tail rotor and into the helicopter.

c. Leave enough room for the tail rotor to spin freely and ensure no glue gets on the rotor.

TOP TIP! Be sure to use minimal glue on the cap for the rotor blade and tail rotor so you don't stick things up. (See TIPS AND TECHNIQUES for more on gluing dowel in place.)

Step 8

a. Drill a hole in the rotor and in the spacer, making sure that the hole is slightly larger than the dowel so it will spin freely.

b. Place a small amount of glue in the top hole in the chopper body and on the bottom of the spacer.

c. Slide the longer spindle from Step 6 through the rotor and spacer and into the helicopter.

④

⑨

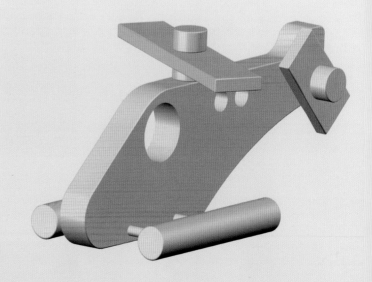

 Paint the helicopter to decorate! (But be careful not to clog up the spinning parts.)

CAR GARAGE

I made this car garage for my son, Gruffydd, when he was three or four years old. And when I saw him call 'Brooom!' with delight as his matchbox car whistled along the little freeway, I remembered just how much I loved playing with my cars as a young bloke too.

Sure, there are options for buying generic garages if you look around, but they are generally plastic or MDF and lack the customised, personalised, strong and durable quality that your homemade service centre will have in spades. Those positives, in addition to the 'you are my hero' look that will come your way, will make this project the most worthwhile of DIY toy constructions and the newest of family heirlooms!

TOOL BOX

Circular saw or handsaw
Clamps
25mm clamping blocks
Drill
12mm drill bit

Hand plane (ideal)
Jigsaw
Palm sander with 80 and
   120 grit sandpaper
Pencil

PVA glue
Square
Straight edge
Tape measure

SHOPPING LIST

Description	Qty	Size	Material
Garage/Signs	1	1200 x 600 x 9	Plywood
Fuel Pumps	1	31 x 19 x 100	Pine
Sign Posts	1	Ø12 x 600	Dowel
Base	1	900 x 600 x 12	Plywood
Nail	41	30 x 2.0	
Treated Pine Screw	6	8g x 30	

THE PLAN

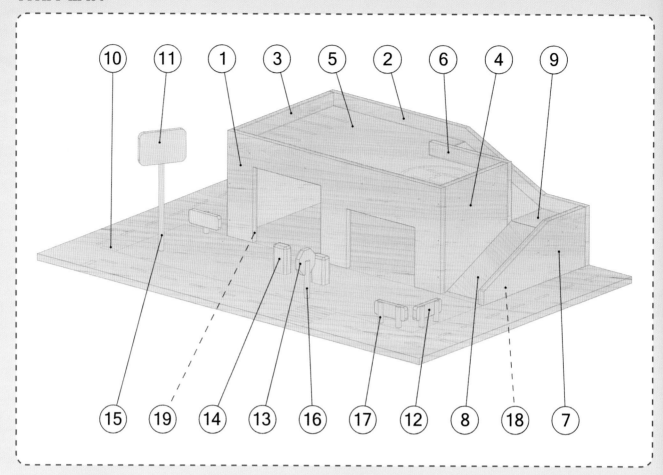

THE PARTS

Part	Description	Qty	Size	Material
1	Front Wall	1	500 x 195 x 9	Plywood
2	Back Wall	1	600 x 195 x 9	Plywood
3	Left Side	1	281 x 195 x 9	Plywood
4	Right Side	1	281 x 195 x 9	Plywood
5	Roof	1	482 x 281 x 9	Plywood
6	Ramp Back	1	185 x 119 x 9	Plywood
7	Ramp Side	1	287 x 110 x 9	Plywood
8	Ramp	2	203 x 91 x 9	Plywood
9	Ramp Platform	1	120 x 91 x 9	Plywood
10	Base	1	900 x 600 x 12	Plywood
11	Large Sign	1	90 x 60 x 9	Plywood
12	Small Sign	3	25 x 70 x 9	Plywood

13	Stop Sign	1	45 x 45 x 9	Plywood
14	Fuel Pump	2	31 x 19 x 50	Pine
15	Long Post	1	Ø12 x 200	Dowel
16	Stop Sign Post	1	Ø12 x 80	Dowel
17	Short Post	5	Ø12 x 50	Dowel
18	Nail	41	30 x 2.0	
19	Treated Pine Screw	6	8g x 30	

MEASURING UP

① Front wall

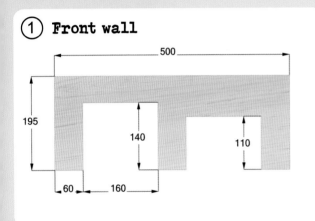

② Back wall

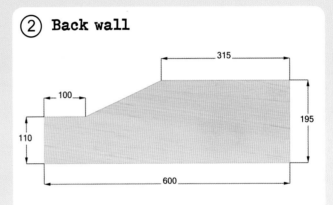

④ Right side

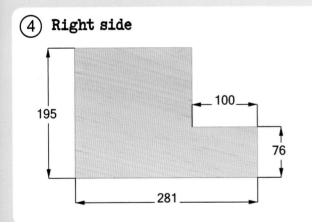

⑤ Roof

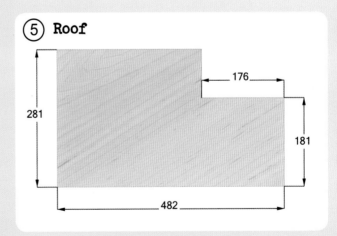

⑥ Ramp back

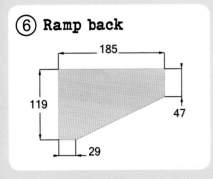

⑦ Ramp side

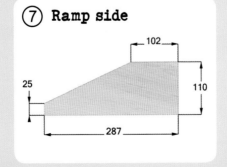

⑧ Ramps

x2

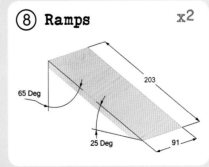

CUTTING GUIDE

It's best to use a circular saw to cut the garage pieces, and tidy the cuts up with a jigsaw, but you can also use a handsaw. See TIPS AND TECHNIQUES for tips on cutting straight lines and cutting corners.

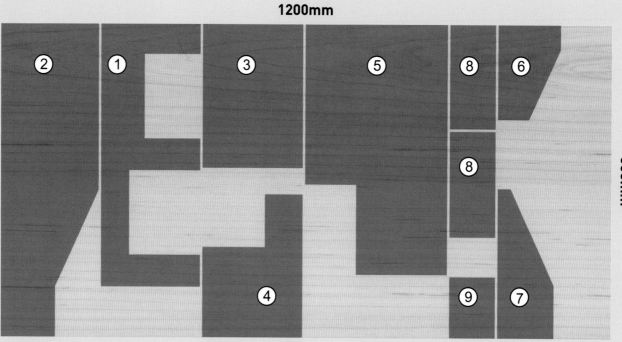

1200mm

600mm

ALTERNATE CUTTING GUIDE

You can arrange the pieces onto a smaller sheet as shown below, but cutting will be more difficult as you cannot run the saw right through each cut.

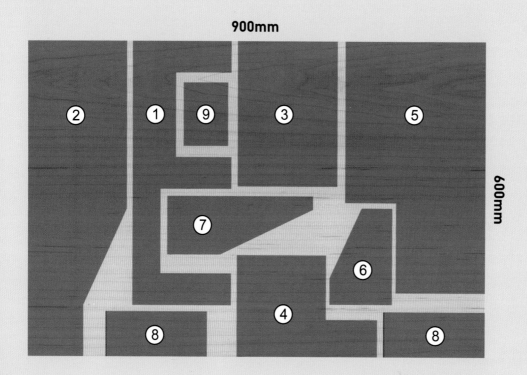

900mm

600mm

INSTRUCTIONS

Step 1

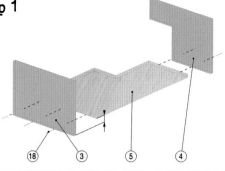

(18) (3) (5) (4)

a. Lying the roof upside down on 25mm blocks and clamping it to the bench will assist in holding the job steady whilst you nail the first two sides in place. Remember to check the sides are square as you nail.

b. Glue and nail both side pieces to the roof. Ensure the front and back edges are flush.

TOP TIP! Many of the steps below show the project rotated to be in position for vertical nailing–horizontal nailing is difficult and inaccurate. Or if you prefer, you can use PVA and hot glue instead of nails for this project.

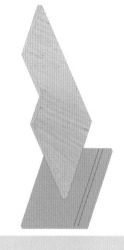

Position where each piece will line up and mark the top and bottom edges. This will give you exactly the right location to drill pilot holes for the nails from the inside.

Step 2

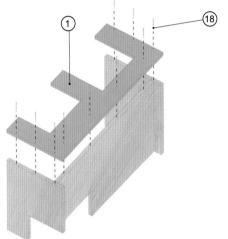

(1) (18)

a. Glue and nail the front wall. Support the garage with spacers after positioning on its side to avoid nailing horizontally.

Step 3

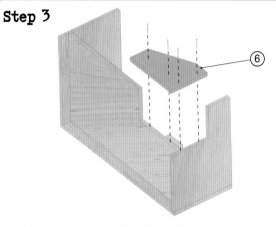

(6)

a. Glue and nail the rear ramp wall.

b. Once in, lay the ramp platform and ramp in position and sketch the edges of the ramp on the outside face.

c. Pre-drill the pilot holes for the ramp (Step 6).

Step 4

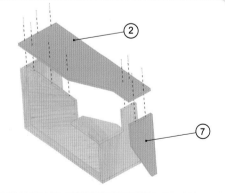

(2) (7)

a. Before adding glue or nails, position the back wall and side ramp wall in place and temporarily fit the ramp again to mark and drill pilot holes (Step 6).

b. Glue and nail the back wall and side ramp wall.

Step 5

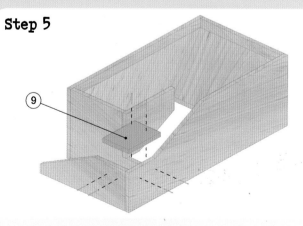

(9)

a. Glue and nail the ramp platform.

b. Add the vertical nails through the platform into the edge of the side piece ④. Make sure the ramp platform is flat before adding the rest of the nails.

Step 6

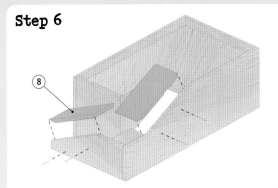

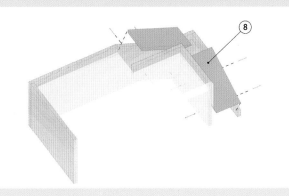

a. Glue and nail the ramps.

b. Only include nails from one side to hold the ramps in place. You may not have drilled pilot holes for the bottom ramp as it is difficult before the ramp corner is in. Do it now but take care, measure the pilot position to align accurately and prevent missing the timber behind.

Step 7

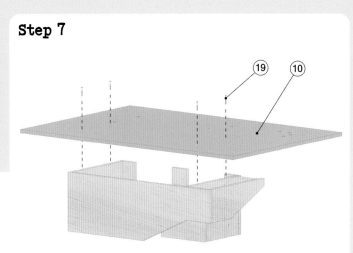

a. Mark the position of the garage and then drill clearance holes for screws in the base.

b. Turn the garage upside down and screw it to the base (remember to drill pilot holes to avoid splitting). Do not use glue so the base can be easily removed if needed.

DECORATION TIME!

Now it's time to put the finishing touches on your new car garage. Make garage signs, road signs, fuel pumps and anything else you can imagine! Remember to look at The Plan on page 22 to remind you of measurements and materials for these final elements.

Step 8

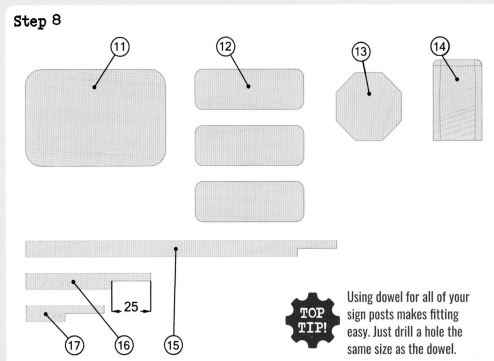

a. Prepare all of the small components and sign pieces.

b. Cut the pieces to size and round all corners. Coarse sandpaper is great for taking the sharpness out of corners, followed by some finer sandpaper to smooth it up nicely.

c. Cut or file 25mm notches in the posts to fit the signs.

TOP TIP! Using dowel for all of your sign posts makes fitting easy. Just drill a hole the same size as the dowel.

Step 9

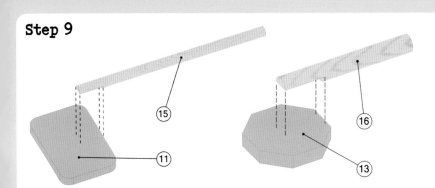

a. Glue the large sign and the stop sign—the hot glue and PVA combo is ideal here.

Step 10

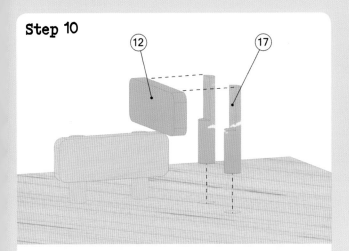

a. Position the small signs and drill the holes to fit the posts.

b. Insert the posts and then glue the signs on.

c. Do not glue in the posts so they can be easily removed if needed.

Step 11

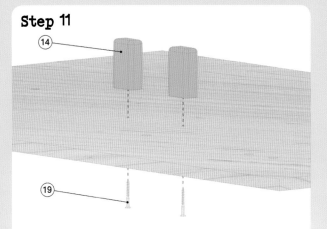

a. Locate the position of the fuel pumps and drill a pilot hole for the screws.

b. Screw in the fuel pumps so they can be removed.

Step 12

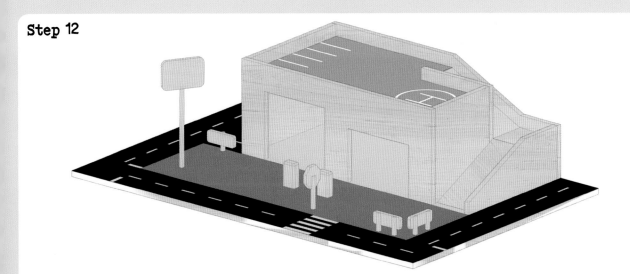

a. Remove all components and sand and prepare for decorating and painting. Painting is much easier if you unscrew the garage from the base and paint it and your signs separately.

b. Paint all pieces the desired colours and add roads, markings, names and so on.

c. Allow to dry before reassembling.

TOP TIP! Paint the base colour first. It is helpful to choose a greyish colour for the base. Call it concrete.
Many less pigmented colours are quite often self-priming so you can knock off two steps in one.
See TIPS AND TECHNIQUES for more on painting.

HOBBY FARM

Who doesn't dream of having a getaway property? Five acres of lush green in a valley surrounded by mountains sounds alright to me.

This hobby farm certainly hit the spot for my five-year-old, Branwen, a couple of years back. She spent countless hours making up games, herding animals and taking miniature families on holidays.

You can go nuts with your surrounding mountain design and no matter what shape you make with your jigsaw, you just make that same shape the horizon of the adjoining mountain side. Don't feel locked in by landscape design either, you can do anything you like—no rules. I did find that keeping the landscape tall in the corner gave me a stronger corner and more room to play around with the papier mâché. Finishing around fence height at the outer edges gave the project a tidy finish and helped to maintain the strength and rigidity in the back walls. Adding hobby grass is a little pricey but so worth it.

Papier mâché is a really simple technique that helps transform three butt-joined pieces of ply into something fun!

TOOL BOX

18mm chisel	Hot glue gun plus	Spray adhesive
Circular saw	glue sticks	Staple gun
Drill	Jigsaw	Straight edge
Drill bits:	Palm sander with 80 and	Tape measure
6mm and 9.5mm	120 grit sandpaper	Wire snips
Hacksaw (for metal)	Pencil	
Hammer	Phillips #2 screwdriver bit	
Handsaw	PVA glue	

SHOPPING LIST

Description	Qty	Size	Material
Frame / Base	1	1200 x 900 x 12	Plywood
Mountain Frame	1	600 x 600	Chicken Wire
Grass	1	1200 x 600	Matting
Fence Posts	2	Ø9.5 x 1200	Dowel
Fence Rail	49	115 x 10 x 2	Ice-Block Stick
Grid	1	Ø6 x 900	Threaded Rod
Grid Frame	1	18 x 18 x 150	Pine
Treated Pine Screw	9	8g x 40	
Newspaper			
Tube Acrylic or Decorative Stones			

THE PLAN

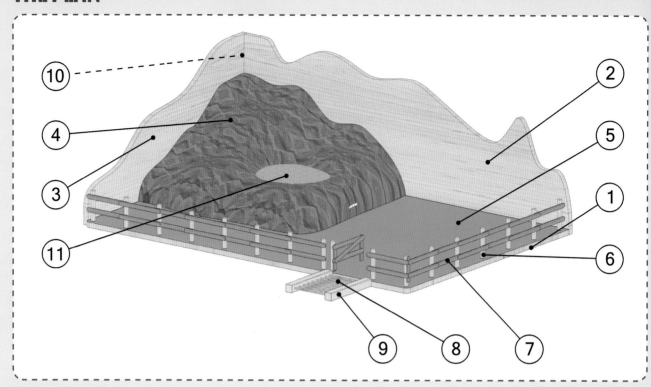

THE PARTS

Part	Description	Qty	Size	Material
1	Base	1	900 x 600 x 12	Plywood
2	Back	1	900 x 300 x 12	Plywood
3	Side	1	600 x 300 x 12	Plywood
4	Mountain Frame	1	600 x 600	Chicken Wire
5	Grass	1	900 x 600	Matting
6	Post	17	Ø9.5 x 80	Dowel
7	Fence Rail	34	115 x 10 x 2	Ice-Block Stick
8	Grid	9	Ø6 x 100	Threaded Rod
9	Grid Frame	2	18 x 18 x 150	Pine
10	Treated Pine Screw	9	8g x 40	
11	Water	1		Acrylic/Resin or Decorative Stones

INSTRUCTIONS

Step 1

Scale 1:10

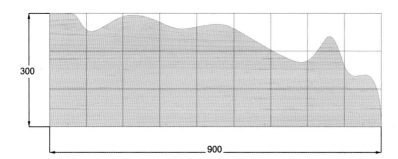

300

900

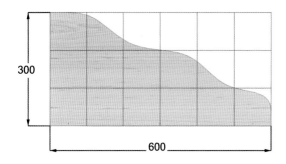

300

600

a. Measure and cut the base from the sheet of plywood.

b. Mark out the shape of the back and side pieces of the frame. Use the grid designs to help.

c. Cut out the shapes with a jigsaw, using a scrolling blade.

d. Clean up all the edges.

Step 2

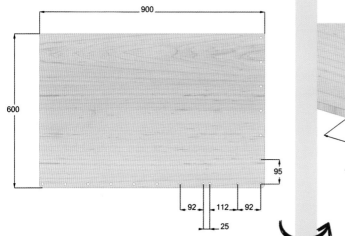

900

600

95

92 112 92

25

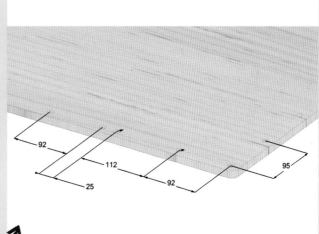

92

112

25

92

95

a. Mark out the positions of the fence post holes and drill them through the base. A 10mm drill bit will work fine for this, if that's all you have.

b. Ice-block sticks may vary in length, so if using a length different to The Parts list, you'll need to adjust the hole spacings to suit what you have. (Lay the gate and fence posts out next to the final locations to check everything will fit.)

The gap for the gate and gate post is bigger to allow for the gate to open and close between gate posts. The gate post needs to pivot freely, so, if needed, wiggle the drill bit slightly as you drill to make the hole slightly larger.

Step 3

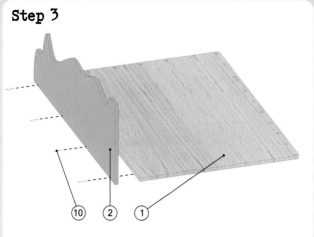

a. Glue and screw the back piece in position (remember to pre-drill). If you'd prefer to be able to take it apart at some point, use screws and no glue.

Step 4

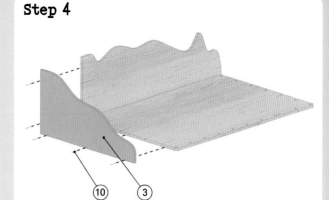

a. Glue and screw the side piece on.

Step 5

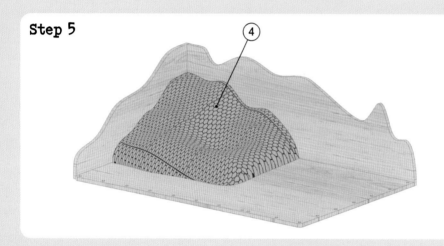

a. Sculpt the chicken wire into a mountainous shape.

b. Allow an edge to be folded under each side so you can staple it in position.

c. Depress a shallow sunken section to become the lake.

d. Make a river if you wish with timber trim.

Step 6

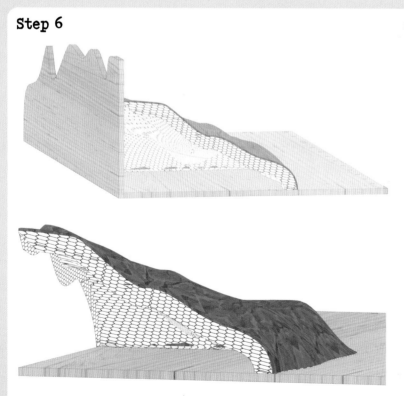

a. Mould the papier mâché over the chicken wire until the desired thickness and surface is obtained.

 There are two techniques I found effective with papier mâché. You can dip individual strips of paper into a PVA glue/water mix. (The water makes the glue runny enough to soak into the paper. The more glue you use the stronger it will be and the quicker it will dry.) Or, you can leave paper in a more-diluted glue mixture overnight, and then make it into a mush in the morning with your hands (gloves are a good idea). The mush allows you to form up odd shapes quickly and easily over your chicken wire–it's more fun, but it takes up to a couple of days to dry, depending how thick it is. I'd recommend a combo of both.

NOW FOR THE BASE!

For sticking on grass matting or hobby grass I'd recommend using contact adhesive in a spray can. Remember, as the name suggests, it sticks on contact so be careful to avoid wrinkles and bubbles. A grass-holding assistant will be a great help, but if you muck it up, never mind, it could be a tree root! I extended the grass up the papier mâché hill—it worked pretty well, though there were a few feature wrinkles in the hill. The choice is yours.

Step 7

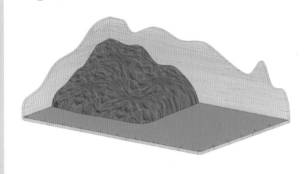

a. Now is the time to have fun with paint. Remember to prime everything first.

b. Add the grass matting to the base (or paint).

Step 8

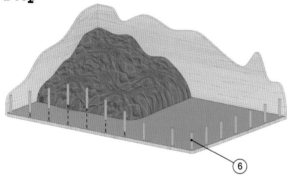

a. Add the fence posts. Push the dowel through the hobby grass into the pre-drilled holes—this will create a snug fit. Glue them in, just don't glue the gate post as you need this to be able to spin.

Step 9

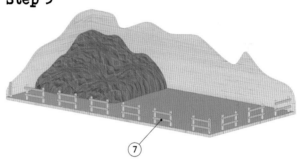

a. Glue the first layer of fence rails on between every second set of posts. Hot glue is a must for this job. You will have it done in minutes.

b. On the end posts, if there is one left, you may want to glue half an ice-block stick to keep the rails even.

c. Now glue the second layer of fence rails in place.

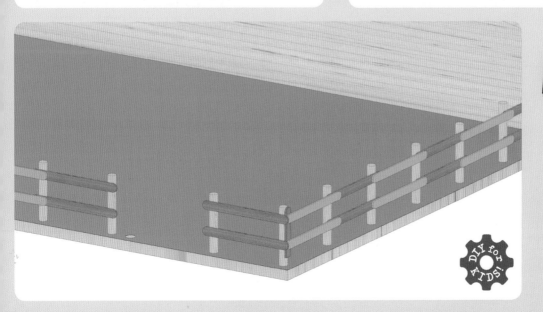

NEXT, BUILD THE GATE!

Step 10

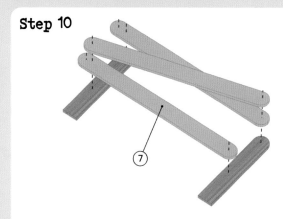

⑦

a. Check sizing of the gate opening before assembling and gluing the gate.

b. Assemble the gate by gluing two ice-block sticks to two half-sticks, and then add one for the diagonal. Fit the diagonal brace last. (Trade tip: the brace always goes from the bottom hinge up to the latch—though no horse has ever complained if it's otherwise!)

Step 11

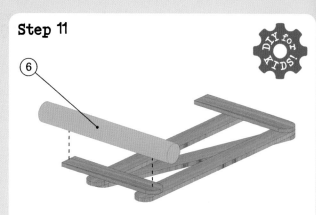

⑥

a. Flip the gate over and glue the gate post on. (A dab of hot glue will help hold it in place while the PVA glue dries.)

AND NOW FOR THE CATTLE GRID...

Step 12

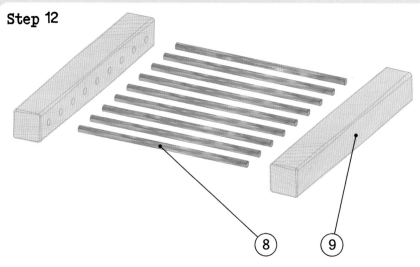

⑧ ⑨

a. Cut the threaded rod into nine 100mm lengths with a hacksaw (you can use your bench hook to cut the threaded rod. Or, even better, clamp it to the bench to hold steady while cutting).

b. Space out nine holes along both grid frame pieces and drill holes halfway through the timbers (see TIPS AND TECHNIQUES for drilling to consistent depths).

c. Glue each length of threaded rod into the holes using PVA glue.

Step 13

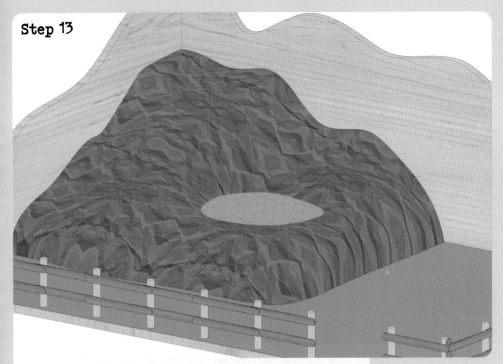

a. Make the water. There are a number of ways to do this. You can use an old tube of acrylic gap sealer and add a bit of blue paint. Spread it around to get a great ripple effect. Or you can use blue decorative stones to make the lake instead—just make sure they are glued securely in place using construction adhesive and PVA glue so they are not a choking hazard. You can find decorative stones in the gardening section of the hardware store.

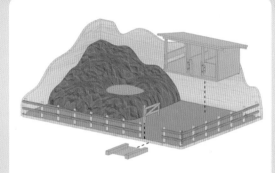

The rest of the components just fit into place, including the stables. (See next project.)

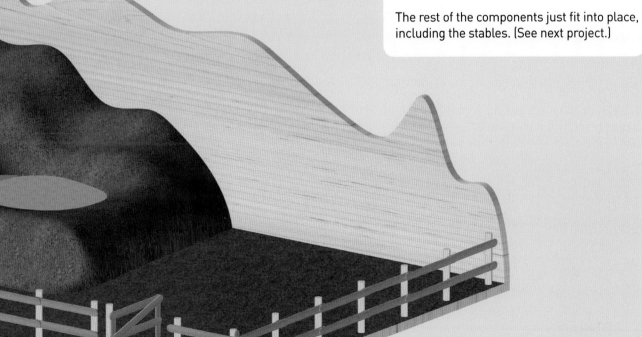

STABLES

If you are going to have a farm, you need to have animals—and those fellas will need a place to call home!

A stable is pretty easy to build, and it will be even easier if you go about it with a hot glue gun. Hot glue gives a near-instant bond, so it is perfect for attaching the small, model-like parts of the stable. The whole assembly takes ten to twenty minutes, tops. And it will be instantly strong enough to decorate and use. Then it's time to bring in the animals!

TOOL BOX

Circular saw
  or drop saw (optional)
Drill
1.5mm drill bit
Handsaw

Hot glue gun plus
  glue sticks
Palm sander with 80 and
  120 grit sandpaper
Pencil

Phillips head screwdriver
PVA glue
Straight edge
Tape measure

SHOPPING LIST

Description	Qty	Size	Material
Panels	1	600 x 450 x 7	Plywood
Frame	2	9 x 9 x 1200	Pine
Hinge	2	35mm	
Wood Screw	8	6g x 12	

THE PLAN

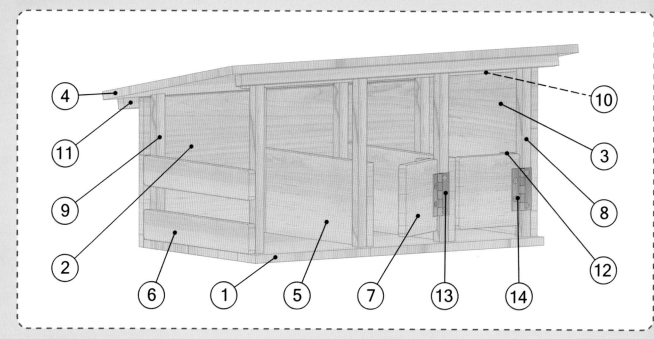

THE PARTS

Part	Description	Qty	Size	Material
1	Base	1	300 x 170 x 7	Plywood
2	Back	1	300 x 125 x 7	Plywood
3	End	1	160 x 150 x 7	Plywood
4	Roof	1	360 x 210 x 7	Plywood
5	Divider	2	160 x 70 x 7	Plywood
6	Rail	2	160 x 25 x 7	Plywood
7	Door	2	65 x 60 x 7	Plywood
8	Front Upright	4	9 x 9 x 150	Pine
9	Back Upright	4	9 x 9 x 122	Pine
10	Top Brace	1	9 x 9 x 290	Pine
11	Roof Support	2	9 x 9 x 330	Pine
12	Door Support	2	9 x 9 x 60	Pine
13	Hinge	2	35mm	
14	Wood Screw	8	6g x 12	

CUTTING GUIDE

Use a circular saw or handsaw to cut out all the stable pieces.

450mm

600mm

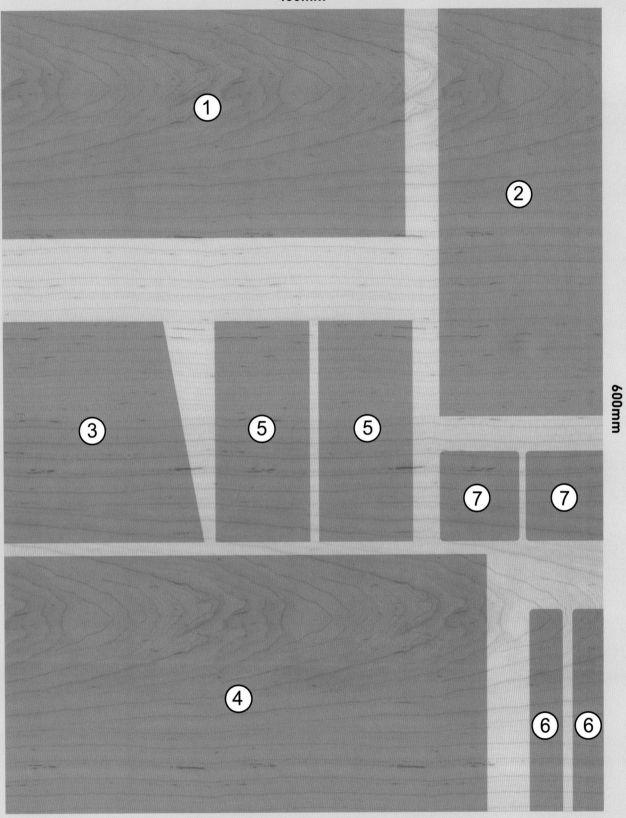

Step 1

Measure and position all of the required pieces on the sheet of plywood and cut them out. Clean up all edges.

Step 2

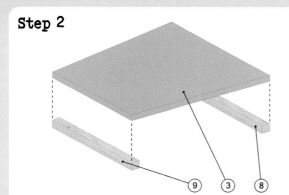

(9) (3) (8)

a. Position the panel end over a front and back upright.
b. Ensure the base and sides are all flush.
c. Trim the uprights to the same angle as the end piece. Transfer this angle to all the other front and back uprights and trim the same.
d. Check which way the plywood is facing so the uprights are on the inside of the frame.
e. Glue the panel to the uprights.

Step 3

x2

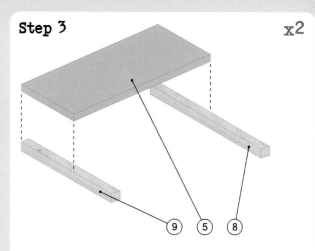

(9) (5) (8)

a. Repeat the process for both the divider sections.

TOP TIP! Too much glue causes the pieces to slide around, making it difficult to position. See TIPS and TECHNIQUES for gluing method when using hot glue and PVA.

Step 4

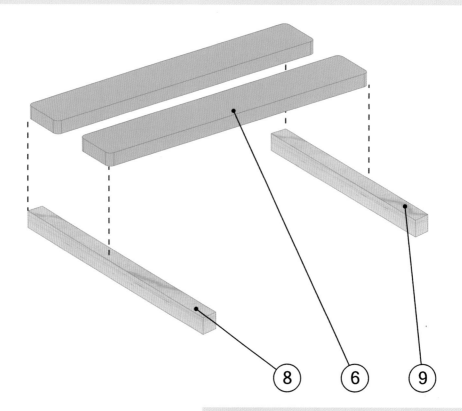

(8) (6) (9)

a. Repeat the process again to add the rails.
b. Leave a 20mm gap between the rails.

DIY for KIDS! Assembling the stable panels in these steps requires no tools, only glue, so it's a great job for DIYers of all ages. Just be sure to supervise the hot glue gun use carefully.

Step 5

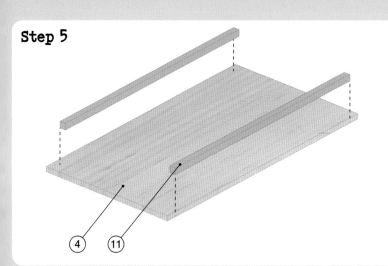

(4) (11)

a. Glue the two roof supports to the roof.

Step 6

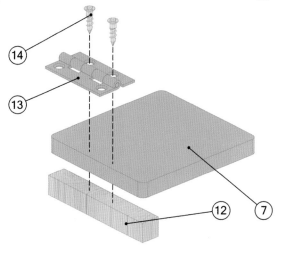

(14)
(13)
(12) (7)

x2

a. Assemble the doors.

b. Glue the door to the door support. Once all of the components are together leave them to dry a little so it is easier to assemble them.

c. Screw the hinge to the front of the door.

d. Repeat the process for the second door.

a. Glue the back panel to the base, using hot glue and PVA.

Step 7

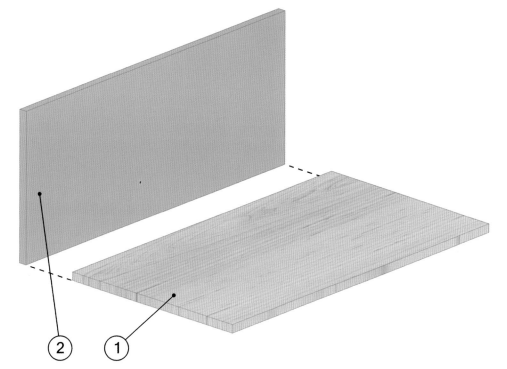

(2) (1)

Step 8

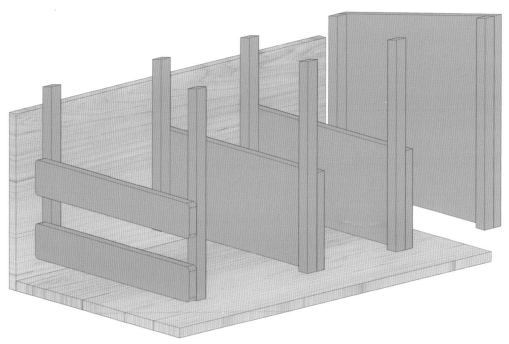

a. Glue the end panel and end railings in place.

b. Check the position of the two middle dividers to make sure the doors will fit and be able to swing, then glue in place.

Step 9

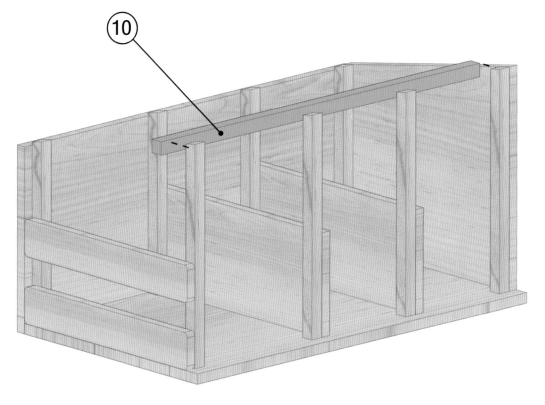

a. Glue on the top brace.

Step 10

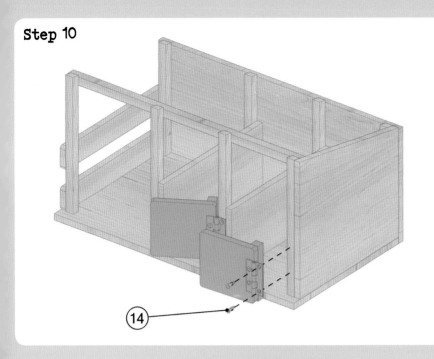

a. Screw the doors in position. Keep the top of the door level with the top of the dividers.

(14)

Step 11

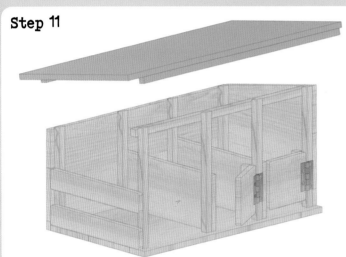

a. Position the roof. It is designed to rest in place.

DIY for KIDS! Paint to decorate!

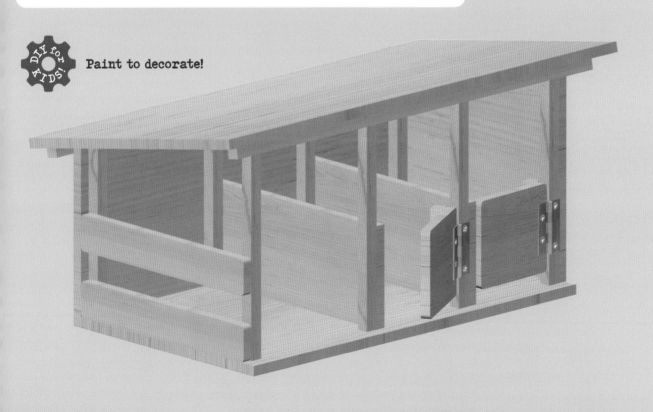

WALL BLOCKS

Some of the best fun I remember having as a kid was targeting my brother's or sister's treasure, behind their wall of defence and under their castle, using mini crossbows and catapults to launch the wooden discs. It was a game that always fired up imaginations—the make-believe battles in the hallway between bedrooms could last for hours at a time!

Recently, I introduced the same game to my own kids. Let's face it, there aren't too many kids that don't get a kick out of building fortresses, defending treasure and demolishing an opposition.

The process of creating this game is quite simple, yet the results are spectacular. I made the blocks out of 18 x 18mm pre-primed pine. This is important, as it's lightweight, cheap and easy to work with. If you make your blocks too big or heavy, the wall will be difficult to break through and knock down.

TOOL BOX

Drill

Handsaw or
   drop saw (ideal)

40mm holesaw

Palm sander with
   80 and 120 grit sandpaper

Pencil

Tape measure (or ruler)

SHOPPING LIST

Description	Qty	Size	Material
Wall	2	18 x 18 x 1200	Pine
Discs	1	68 x 12 x 600	Pine
		or 600 x 300 x 12	Plywood

TOP TIP! This will make enough blocks for one wall.
Adjust the quantities for your own requirements.

THE PLAN

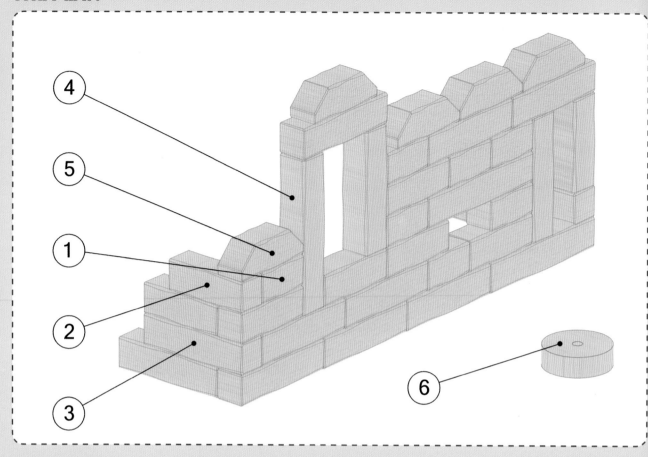

THE PARTS

The best lengths for the blocks are multiples of the section width of the 18mm timber so they stack evenly. In this case, 36mm, 54mm, 72mm and 90mm.

Part	Description	Qty	Size	Material
1	2-Length Block	9	18 x 18 x 36	Pine
2	3-Length Block	10	18 x 18 x 54	Pine
3	4-Length Block	13	18 x 18 x 72	Pine
4	5-Length Block	3	18 x 18 x 90	Pine
5	3-Length Block Turret	5	18 x 18 x 54	Pine
6	Disc	20–50	Ø40 x 12	Pine/Plywood

INSTRUCTIONS

Step 1

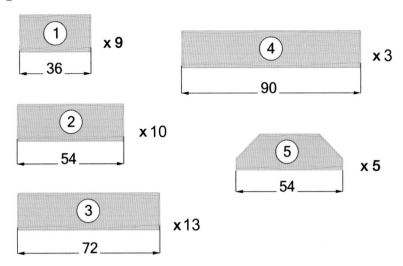

① x 9
36

④ x 3
90

② x 10
54

⑤ x 5
54

③ x 13
72

a. Cut the timber into block lengths.

b. Cut a 45 degree angle on the ends of the turret blocks to use as the top battlements.

c. Sand the edges of the blocks.

TOP TIP!

A palm sander is great for buzzing off the corners of each block, to make the edges softer.

If you rub the corner of the blocks on some driveway concrete before sanding, it removes the sharpness on the corners and makes the blocks easy to palm-sand smooth without tearing the sandpaper.

DIY for KIDS!

Step 2

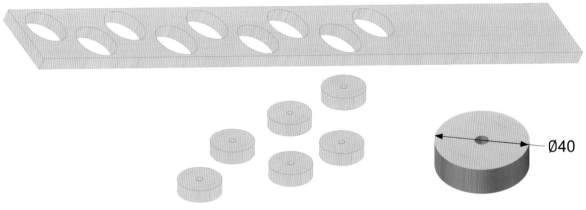

Ø40

a. Use a 40mm holesaw to cut out a series of discs to use for ammunition.

b. Sand the edges. Remember, these are battle discs—any imperfections in shape and smoothness is quite acceptable.

Step 3

These discs work with the next two projects, the Crossbow and Catapault.

a. Paint the blocks. If you lay all the blocks down together on a board, painting is quick and easy with spray cans. Incline the board as much as you can towards vertical without the blocks sliding off. An upright spray can is much easier to use and more efficient.

DIY for KIDS!

CROSSBOW

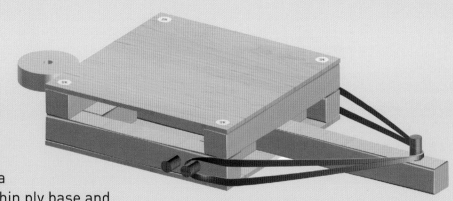

The crossbow is a pretty simple project also—and perfect for launching the ammunition discs across the floor towards the enemy block wall!

The crossbow has a firing rod that is pulled forward by a rubber band. A masonite or thin ply base and lid contains the whole mechanism, and ensures no-one pinches their finger. Dowel pieces added to the firing rod will restrict the loading and firing capabilities. The crossbow is fired from the ground. One hand is needed to hold the mechanism and the other to pull back the firing rod aimed at the ordinance discs.

If you want your crossbow to stay in optimum condition, it's best to use hardwood for the firing rod, front cross piece and the dowel. During use, these pieces hit into each other, so soft pine will gradually bruise and work loose over time.

TOOL BOX

Drill
Drill bits: 3mm and 5mm
Hammer
Handsaw or drop saw
 (ideal, but not essential)

Palm sander with
 80 and 120 grit sandpaper
Pencil
Phillips head screwdriver
 or screwdriver bit

PVA glue
Tape measure (or ruler)

SHOPPING LIST

Description	Qty	Size	Material
Base / Top	1	300 x 150 x 3	Plywood or Masonite
Frame	1	18 x 18 x 1200	Pine or Hardwood
Pins	1	Ø8 x 1200	Dowel
Wood Screw	4	8g x 35	
Brad	14	10 x 1.0	
Rubberband	1		

THE PLAN

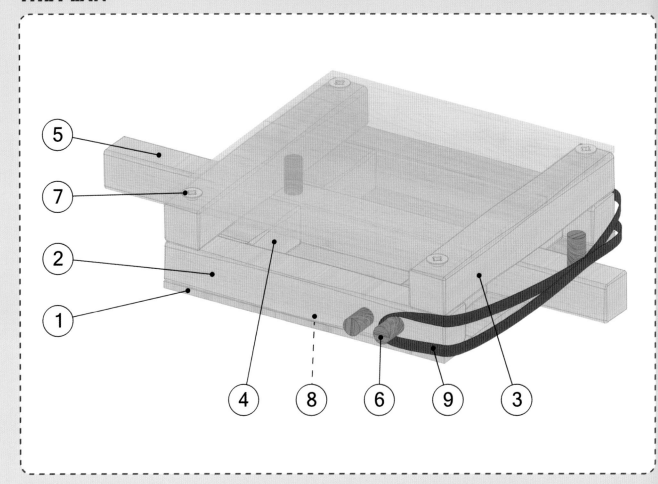

THE PARTS

Part	Description	Qty	Size	Material
1	Base / Top	2	140 x 140 x 3	Plywood or Masonite
2	Frame	2	18 x 18 x 140	Pine or Hardwood
3	Top Frame	2	18 x 18 x 140	Pine or Hardwood
4	Spacer	4	18 x 18 x 42	Pine or Hardwood
5	Firing Rod	1	18 x 18 x 250	Pine or Hardwood
6	Pin	6	Ø8 x 30	Dowel
7	Wood Screw	4	8g x 35	
8	Brad	14	10 x 1.0	
9	Rubberband	1		

INSTRUCTIONS

Step 1

a. Cut all the pieces to size.

Step 2 x2

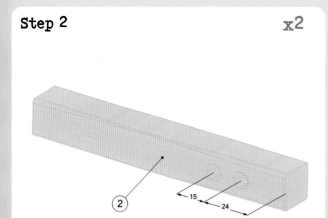

a. Drill two holes in the side frame pieces to firmly fit the dowel pins. (See TIPS AND TECHNIQUES for tips on how to drill into small pieces of timber.)

Step 3

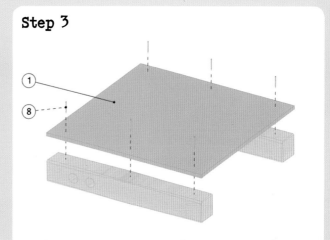

a. Glue and nail the base to the frame pieces, ensuring the nails do not interfere with the dowel holes.

Step 4

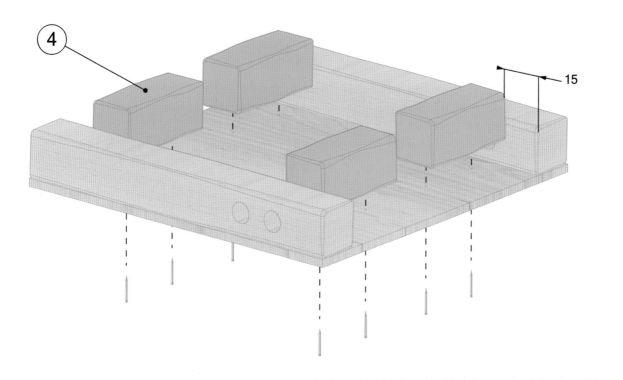

a. Attach the spacers. Because the spacers will be underneath and hard to see while nailing, tap the nails just through the base first to help position them accurately before finishing off the nails.

Step 5

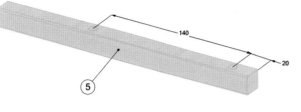

a. Drill two holes into the firing rod, to a depth of 15mm, to fit the stop pins. The position of these holes is important to prevent the firing rod pulling past the guide spacers. Do not drill these all the way through to keep a smooth base.

b. If necessary, sand or plane 1mm off each of two faces of the firing rod to ensure it is slightly smaller than the gap provided by the frame you have made. You want the rod to slide smoothly through the gap without obstruction.

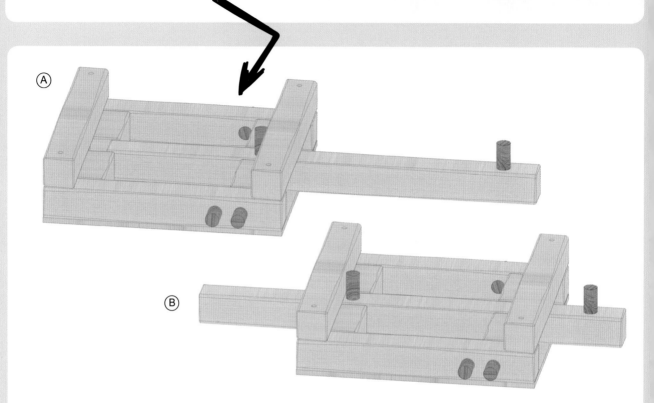

The internal stop controls the position of the firing rod. When retracted (position Ⓐ), the front of the firing rod should not pull past the spacers as this will cause a misfire. When released (position Ⓑ) it will hit the front guard and stop the hook pin short of the rear guard to prevent pinching.

Step 6

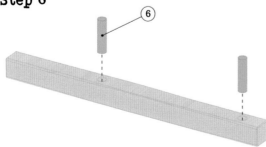

a. Insert the dowel pins. These pins will bear the brunt of the force so it is better to glue them in place.

Step 7

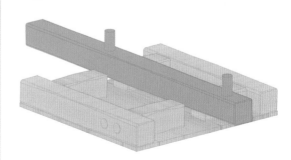

a. Locate the firing rod in place.

b. Check it slides freely in between the guide spacers.

Step 8

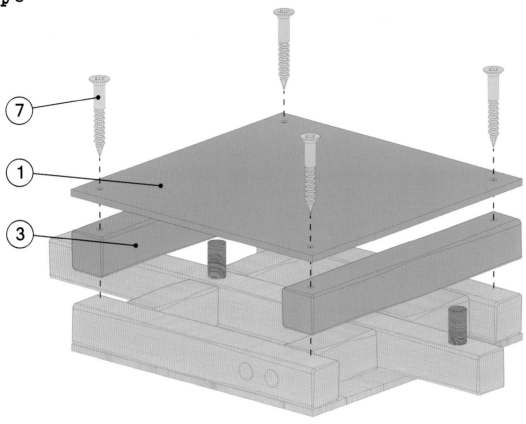

(7)

(1)

(3)

a. Assemble the rest of the frame.

b. Drill pilot holes for the screws to prevent splitting and countersink to the top. Remember clearance holes in the three pieces shown above in blue.

Step 9

a. Insert the pins to hold the rubber band.

b. Stretch the band across the back of the crossbow. You can add more pins or screws depending on the size of the rubber band.

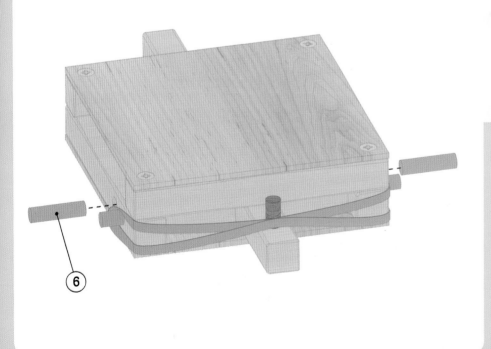

(6)

CATAPAULT

The catapult is basically a simple frame with one moving or pivoting arm that throws an object.

Most of the base frame is made out of the same 18 x 18mm pine used to create the wall blocks, with the exception of the front piece. This axle is made using dowel so that a throwing arm can be connected via a hole at one end, slightly bigger than the dowel, allowing it to pivot freely. A hole at the other end of the throwing arm allows a rubber band to pass through.

To create a holding tray at the top of the throwing arm, simply take a plastic lid or cut the bottom of a plastic bottle, at least 50mm in diameter, and screw it to the throwing arm. Your catapult is ready for battle!

TOOL BOX

Drop saw (ideal, but not essential)
Drill
Drill bits:
  3mm, 5mm and 9.5mm
Hammer

Handsaw
Palm sander with
  80 and 120 grit sandpaper
Phillips head screwdriver
  or screwdriver bit
Pencil

PVA glue
Tape measure (or ruler)

SHOPPING LIST

Description	Qty	Size	Material
Base	1	236 x 200 x 3	Plywood
Frame	1	18 x 18 x 1800	Pine
Axle	1	Ø9.5 x 236	Dowel
Wood Screw	6	8g x 35	
Wood Screw	3	8g x 25	
Bottle Base	1	Approx. Ø60	Plastic
Rubberband	1		
Washer	1	5mm	
Brad	9	10 x 1.0	

THE PLAN

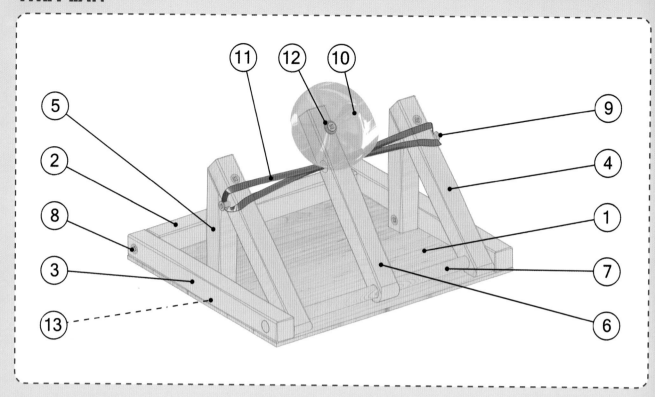

THE PARTS

Part	Description	Qty	Size	Material
1	Base	1	236 x 200 x 3	Plywood
2	Back	1	18 x 18 x 200	Pine
3	Side	2	18 x 18 x 200	Pine
4	Diagonal Brace	2	18 x 18 x 160	Pine
5	Riser	2	18 x 18 x 100	Pine
6	Throw Arm	1	18 x 18 x 180	Pine
7	Axle	1	Ø9.5 x 236	Dowel
8	Wood Screw	6	8g x 35	
9	Wood Screw	3	8g x 25	
10	Bottle Base	1	Approx. Ø60	Plastic
11	Rubberband	1		
12	Washer	1	5mm	
13	Brad	9	10 x 1.0	

INSTRUCTIONS

Step 1   a.   Gather all pieces and components. Cut to size as required.

Step 2

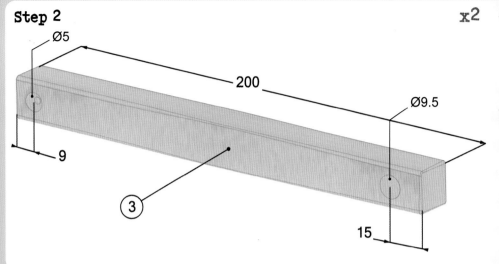

Ø5
200
Ø9.5
9
15
3

x2
a. Drill a 5mm clearance hole for the screw into the base side piece (remember to countersink).

b. Drill the hole for the dowel. Ideally, the dowel holes should be the same size as the dowel for a firm fit. A 10mm drill bit will be fine if that's all you have, just be sure to glue it well.

Step 3

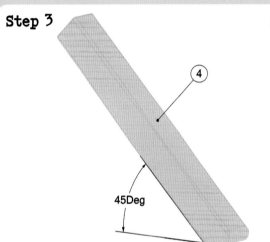

4
45Deg

x2
a. Cut the two diagonal braces. Start with the piece at the correct length, then cut the base at a 45 degree angle, before rounding the corner.

Step 5   **x2**

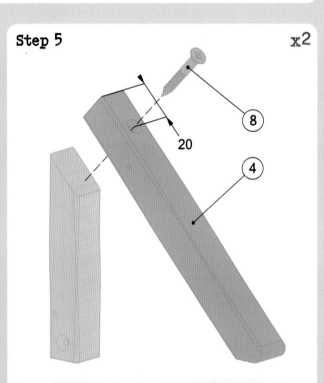

8
20
4

a. Assemble the two riser frames.

b. Position the two pieces together and pre-drill a pilot hole in the riser to help align the screw. Then drill a clearance hole in the diagonal brace and countersink the hole to prevent splitting the timber. (See TIPS AND TECHNIQUES for more tips on screws.)

Step 4

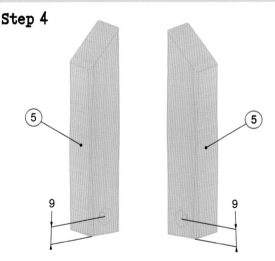

5   5
9   9

a. Drill a 5mm clearance hole in both risers, and countersink, to avoid splitting. Ensure you do this on different sides for the left and right risers.

Step 6

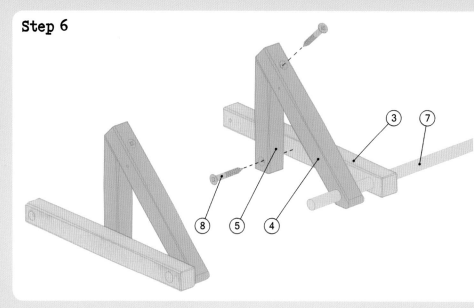

a. Attach the riser frames to the side pieces.

b. Drill the holes for the axle through both diagonal braces and side pieces.

Step 7

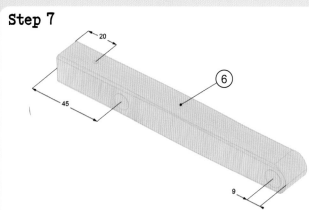

a. Drill the hole for the rubber band into the throw arm.

b. Round the other end of the throw arm so that the arm can pivot on the axle.

c. Drill the hole for the axle into the rounded end of the throw arm. Use a drill bit that is the same size as the dowel, but wiggle it a little as you drill to make the axle hole slightly larger. This will allow the throw arm to spin freely on the dowel. Using a larger drill bit for the hole will make the throw arm very loose.

Step 8

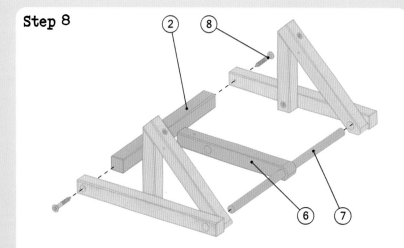

a. Slide the throw arm over the dowel as you locate the axle in position, checking that the rounded end enables the throw arm to move freely before fixing permanently in place.

b. Tap the axle into place, position the throw arm in the centre, and slide each side piece on, from either end of the axle. Use PVA at the end joins (but be sure to keep any glue away from the throw arm as it needs to move freely). The dowel will fit snugly at both ends of the frame so use a hammer and a block of timber to lift the catapult off the bench. You may need to twist the frame slightly to help the dowel into position. Tap the dowel through until the end you are hitting is just clear of the inside of the catapult frame. Then turn the catapult over and tap from the other end, using a timber block as a spreader if necessary, until both ends of the dowel finish flush with the outside edge of the frame.

c. Position the back piece in place between the side pieces and attach.

Step 9

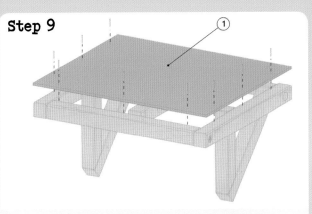

a. Glue and nail the base. Make sure you have support under the piece you are nailing. You could hang the frame over the edge of a bench or rest each side on a scrap piece of timber.

Step 10

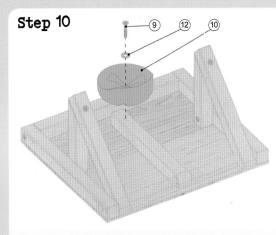

a. Cut the base off a PET bottle and sand the edges clean. Cutting the bottle base with a turn up at the bottom will give the disc somewhere to sit (but don't include a turn up at the top or it will interfere with the slinging action of the disc).

b. Attach the bottle base to the throw arm with a screw and a small washer.

Step 11

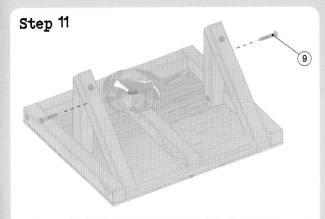

a. Add a screw on each diagonal brace for the rubber band to hook on to.

Step 12

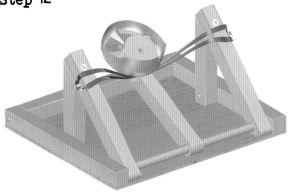

a. Feed the rubber band through the hole in the throwing arm and hook over the screws.

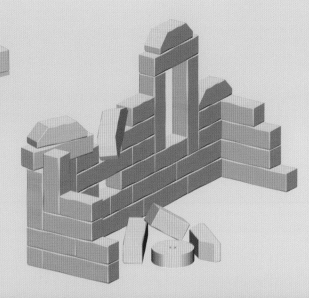

BACKYARD GAMES

BACKYARD GAMES

MAYPOLE

My sister was turning eight on the 1st of May a few years back. Dad came up with a cracker idea for a maypole that didn't just provide a great party game spectacle, but also looked brilliant in the yard both before and after the party.

When your maypole is constructed (I found using a cardboard tube from a roll of carpet works best—they're available from carpet suppliers for free if you ask nicely!), kids will have loads of fun weaving in and out to music trying to make as neat a weave as possible. Once weaving humans becomes impossible (it's a lot of fun to watch), simply turn the kids around and reverse the weave. The laughs are well worth the effort to make this one and once you have the pole you can set it up anywhere very simply—the backyard, the park or anywhere you want to combine kids, colour and fun!

TOOL BOX

Adjustable wrench	**Hammer** (lump hammer	**PVA glue**
Drill	is helpful)	**Saw horses**
6mm drill bit	**Handsaw**	**Tape measure** (or ruler)
Duct tape	**Pencil**	

SHOPPING LIST

Description	Qty	Size	Material
Tube	1	Ø100 x 3000	Cardboard or Plastic
Star Picket	2	1650	Steel
Crown	4	20 x 8 x 600	Tasmanian Oak or Pine
Cup Head Bolt	1	M6 x 50	Galvanised
Ribbon	8	7m lengths in different colours	

Plastic Flowers or Other Decoration

INSTRUCTIONS

Step 1   a.   Paint the cardboard tube. I find that grey is a good base colour to use under the bright coloured ribbon though any colour will do. The paint helps to protect the cardboard. Exterior paint is ideal but not really that important. Use paint you have at home to reduce cost.

Step 2

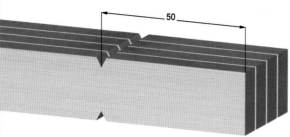

a. Cut the crown pieces to size, four pieces each 600mm long.

b. Then cut notches, 50mm in from both ends of each piece. (Tip: lay the four pieces together against your bench hook and make two small cuts in a V-shape that continues across all four pieces.) Turn the timber pieces over and repeat. Then do the same at the other end.

Step 3

a. Stack the four crown pieces and drill a hole through the centre of all pieces for the cup head machine bolt. Drilling is easier when the pieces are neatly stacked, with all ends and edges lined up. And clamping will ensure nothing moves as you drill.

b. Add PVA glue and stack the pieces over the bolt. As you stack, spin the first two pieces to create a cross and then the following two to create a wheel of spokes.

Step 4

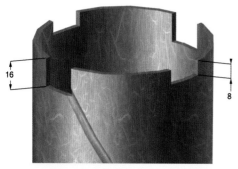

a. Cut four 20mm housings or notches into the top of the cardboard tube, to fit the width of the crown pieces. Two of the housings will be 16mm deep and opposite each other. Two will be 8mm deep and opposite each other. They are equally spaced around the rim for the four lowest crown pieces to fit into. This helps to stabilise the crown when it is in position.

Step 5

a. Tape the timber crown pieces to the top rim of the cardboard using duct tape or similar. Tie the pieces of ribbon to the crown spokes at the notch locations. Add additional decorations, like flowers, to the top of the crown, if you like. Plastic flowers have plenty of colour, are pretty cheap and last for ages.

Step 6

a. Hammer the steel star pickets into the ground in the centre of a large outdoor area. The tip is to have the pickets close to each other at the base, so the pole can just slide over them. Lean the pickets out slightly as you drive them in using a hammer. You will need to pull the pickets in at the top to get them close enough for the pole to fit over them. Release the pickets gradually as the pole slides over them—the pickets will spring outwards creating pressure on the inside edges of the pole helping to hold it steady without any wobbles.

b. Pull the ribbon into different positions around the pole and hold each in place with a rock or similar.

SKITTLES

I'm honestly not sure if this game is easier to make or to play. These skittles are pretty compact and can be used anywhere. The first time we used them was on a camping trip and they hit the mark straightaway.

Anyone can play and, with a bit of simple addition, you can score. Stand them up with space between each one and the idea is to knock over the timbers and add the total score. You can make your own rules but I always start with a first to 21 game. If the score goes over 21, then minus the excess from 21. You need an exact score to finish.

The more you spread out the skittles the harder it is to start, but it is easier to finish by hitting only the one you want. The throwing object? The best I could think of was a newel post cap. You know those knobs that sit on the post at the bottom of a set of stairs? Well they are round at one point but irregular everywhere else so they can bounce anywhere. Hard to predict and they make for a much more fun game than using just a ball.

TOOL BOX

Clamp	**Handsaw**	**Phillips head screwdriver**
Drop saw (ideal, but not essential)	**Palm sander** with 80 and 120 grit sandpaper	or screwdriver bit
Drill	**Pencil**	**PVA glue**
1.5mm drill bit		**Tape measure** (or ruler)

SHOPPING LIST

Description	Qty	Size	Material
Box*	1	140 x 19 x 1800	Pine
Skittles	2	70 x 35 x 1200	Pine
Newel Cap	4	Ø100	Pine
Nail	18	50 x 2.0	
Number	11		Self-Adhesive Numeral

* Making the box is optional—but it does make the skittles easier to carry around.

THE PLAN

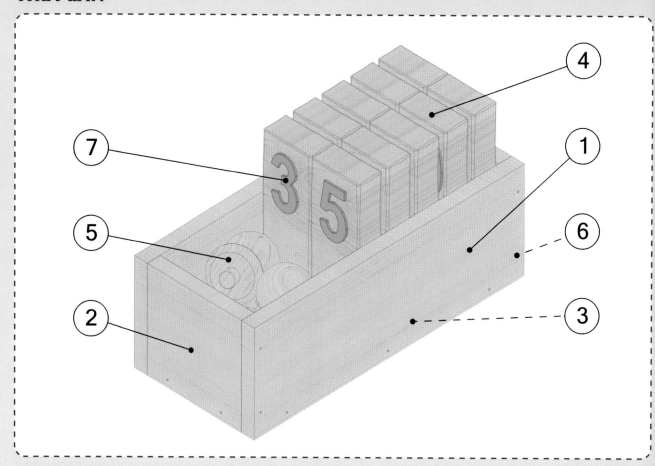

THE PARTS

Part	Description	Qty	Size	Material
1	Side	2	140 x 19 x 400	Pine
2	End	2	140 x 19 x 140	Pine
3	Base	1	140 x 19 x 362	Pine
4	Skittle	10	70 x 35 x 200	Pine
5	Newel Cap	4	Ø100	Pine
6	Nail	18	50 x 2.0	Pine
7	Number	11		Self-Adhesive Numeral

INSTRUCTIONS

Step 1

a. Cut the pieces of timber for the skittles. You can cut as many skittles as you like for the game, but ten is generally a good number.

b. Sand and then paint to decorate.

Step 2

x10

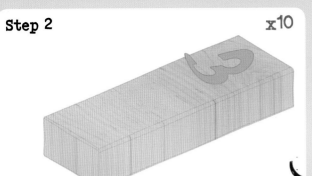

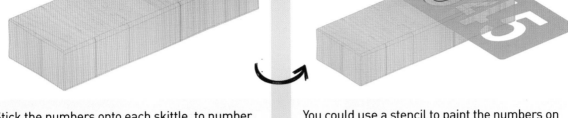

a. Stick the numbers onto each skittle, to number from 1 to 10.

You could use a stencil to paint the numbers on each skittle, or just draw them on too.

Step 3

a. For the bombs, you can be creative and use anything that will knock the skittles down. But for something easy to find, and that has an unpredictable bounce, a set of newel caps are ideal. Paint to decorate.

Step 4

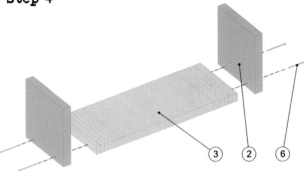

a. To make the skittles storage box, measure and cut the pieces for the base, ends and sides. (You can adjust the size of the box if required.)

b. Pre-drill 1.5mm pilot holes into the end pieces ② and side pieces ①.

c. Clamp the base piece to the bench with the edge that requires nailing close to the edge of the bench. This will make driving the nails horizontally easier.

d. Glue and nail the ends on to the base.

Step 5

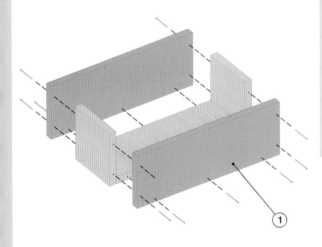

a. Glue and nail both sides to the base. Make sure to rotate the box so that you can nail vertically—it helps a lot.

b. Sand to clean up and then paint to decorate.

BOX KITE

It amazes me how little wind is required to launch this beauty. I have built many of them in the past, and have even been able to get them flying indoors just by running around!

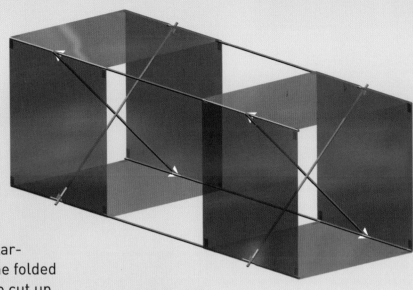

The kites are pretty simple to make, especially if you follow a couple of important tips.

The best bags to use are regular-sized gardening bags, which come folded flat. The folded bags are easier to cut up. (I get them in orange, which adds that all-important colour.)

And make sure you get any barcode stickers off your dowel and give it a sand before sliding on the hose connectors—that sticky stuff makes getting the hose on a real chore. Sitting the hose pieces in some hot water briefly before sliding them into place also makes the job easy.

Then all you have to do is add your plastic and some string and start running!

TOOL BOX

Handsaw	Scissors
Marker pen	Straight edge
Pencil	Tape measure
Pliers	Utility knife

SHOPPING LIST

Description	Qty	Size	Material
Frame	6	Ø6 x 1200	Dowel
Connectors	1	Ø6 x 1000	Clear Vinyl Tubing*
Garden Bag	1	800 x 1200	
Roll Tape	1		
Kite String (optional)	1	30m	Lightweight String or Nylon Builders Line

* You will most likely need to buy the tubing in a 2–5m length, which will leave you with extra—for more kites you can make!

THE PLAN

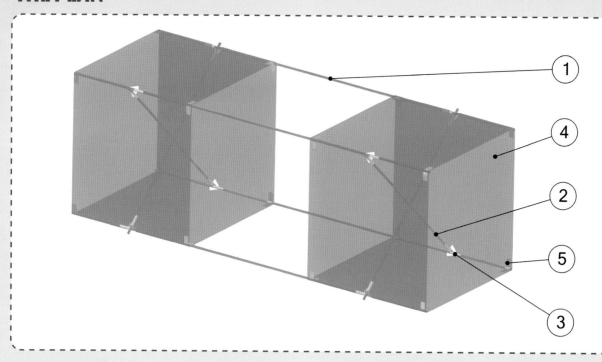

THE PARTS

Part	Description	Qty	Size	Material
1	Frame	4	Ø6 x 1200	Dowel
2	Braces	4	Ø6 x 600	Dowel
3	Connectors	8	Ø6 x 70	Vinyl Tube
4	Garden Bag	1	800 x 1200	
5	Tape	1		

INSTRUCTIONS

Step 1   x8

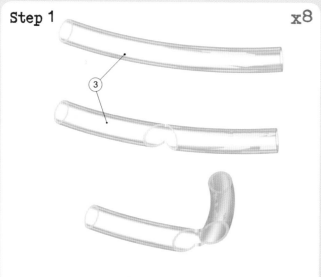

a. Using a sharp utility knife, cut the eight tubes to length.

b. Cut a notch halfway across the middle of each tube so that they can bend to 90 degrees.

Step 2   x8

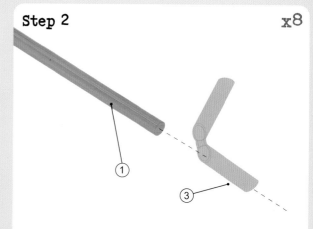

a. Fit a tube over both ends of the four long frame pieces. The hose can sometimes be tight and difficult to slide. Either warm the tube in hot water first, or use pliers to help push the tube on the dowel.

b. Adjust to have the tubes facing the same way.

Step 3

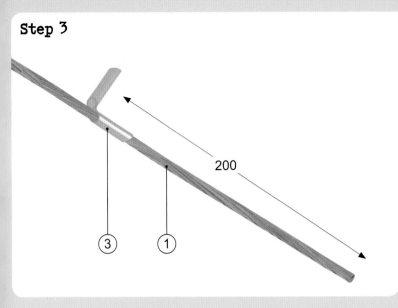

200

③ ①

a. Slide each tube into position about 200mm from the ends of the long dowel pieces. They will provide a T-section joint for the diagonal bracing pieces to connect at 90 degrees (but don't join the bracing pieces until Step 10). Pliers will help position the tube onto the dowel, if you push on the square cut end of the tube as it slides down the dowel.

Once the dowel and tube lengths are cut to size, kids can help with the assembling all the parts!

Step 4

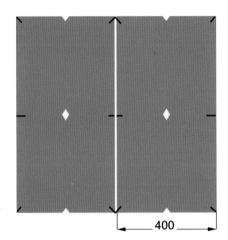

400

a. Lay the garbage bag flat. The more folded the bag remains, the easier the cutting process is.

b. Cut off the closed end of the bag.

c. Measure and cut two 400mm sections. You will have two giant calamari rings of plastic. Keep them flat for now.

d. Cut a triangular notch halfway along each folded end, and cut a diamond-shaped notch in the centre of the top and bottom layers of each piece.

e. Use a marker pen to mark halfway along on the edges of each piece so you can easily line up the dowel in Step 5. Mark both sides of the plastic at all corners and the inside and outside of both the top and bottom layers at the centre of each piece.

Step 5

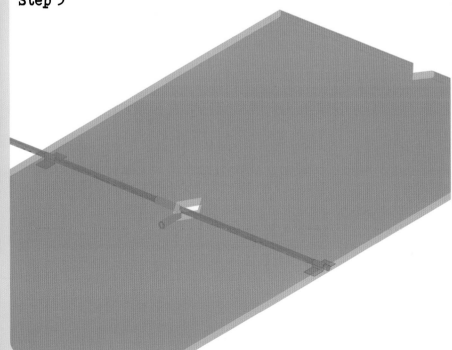

a. Get sixteen 50mm lengths of tape ready on the edge of the table—it will make taping easier.

b. Insert the first length of dowel in between the top and bottom plastic layers.

c. Line the end of the dowel up with the outside edge in line with the mark and tape it down. Stretch the plastic tight, line up with the inside edge mark and tape it down. The plastic tube connector should be in line with the hole in the middle of the plastic.

Step 6

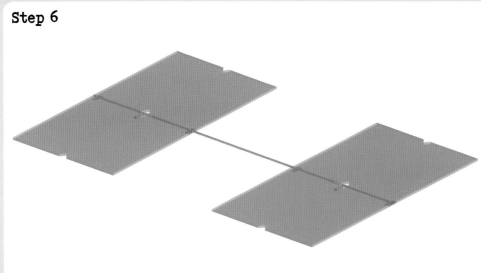

a. Repeat the taping process with the other plastic sleeve, taping it to the other end of the long dowel piece. This will ensure that you maintain an even space of about 400mm between the two plastic sections.

Step 7

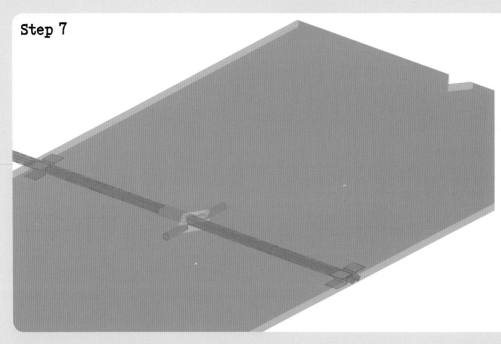

a. Pick up the two plastic sleeves and flip them over like a pancake to work on the other side.

b. Repeat Step 5 and Step 6 with the second piece of dowel, close to the first, taping down to the underneath layer of plastic.

Step 8

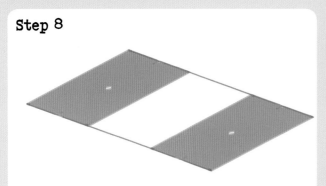

a. Here is where you can start to impress the kids! Hold each piece of dowel and pull them apart so that both dowels end up at the outside edge. The diamond holes in the middle should align.

Step 9

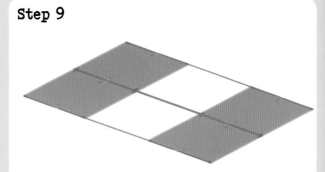

a. Repeat Steps 5–7 to add the remaining two lengths of dowel.

Step 10

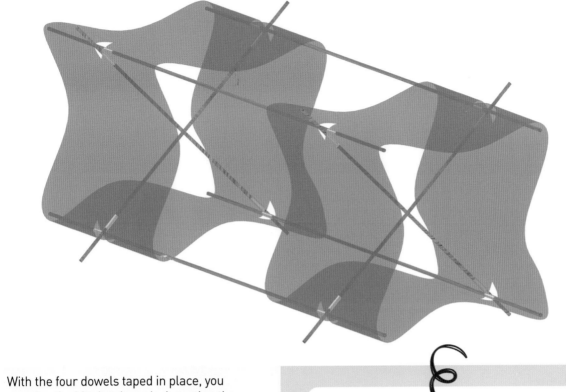

a. With the four dowels taped in place, you can give the kite its shape by inserting the diagonal braces into the tube connectors.

b. It is slightly awkward, but insert the dowel from the inside of each plastic box section. Slide the dowel through the tube more than seems necessary (pliers used as a stop on the edge of the tubing allowing the dowel to pass through will help, though be careful not to tear the plastic or the tube). Over-feeding the first part of the dowel allows easier fitting of the other end, as the plastic will be more slack.

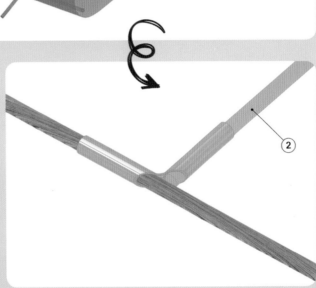

2

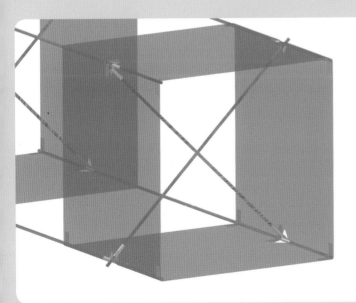

Step 11

a. Once all the dowel is connected, gently push the tubing towards the ends of the diagonal pieces to tension the kite.

b. Tie the kite string to any point where the diagonal braces meet the mainframe at a plastic joint.

You can add a tail to the bottom of the kite if you want to be flash, but the kite will fly beautifully without it!

FOOTY GOAL

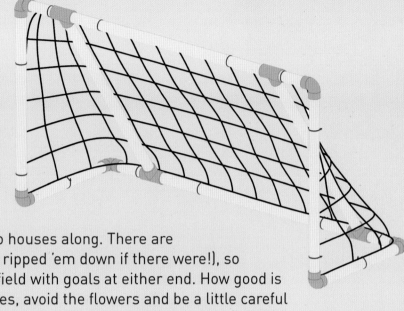

Given half a chance, kids deadset love running around the yard. Throw in a bit of healthy competition in the form of a goal target, and these footy goals will turn your backyard, or any patch of grass, into a sporting arena!

We have mates that get on so well with their neighbours that they put one set of goals in their front yard and the other set in the front yard two houses along. There are no fences between them (they'd have ripped 'em down if there were!), so effectively they have a 40-odd metre field with goals at either end. How good is that? They do have to dodge a few trees, avoid the flowers and be a little careful over the three concrete driveways in between, but hey . . . that's all part of the beauty of DIY home footy! Play on!!

TOOL BOX

Handsaw or hacksaw	**Tape measure**
Pencil	**Utility knife**
PVC cement	

SHOPPING LIST

Description	Qty	Size	Material
Frame	4*	Ø40 x 3m	PVC Pipe
Tee	6	40mm	PVC
Elbow	2*	40mm	PVC
Inspection Elbow	2	40mm	PVC
End Cap	2	40mm	PVC
Net	1	2.4m x 1.2m	
Cable Tie	14	200mm	

* If making a soccer goal only, you will need two additional elbows in place of two of the tees, and only three lengths of PVC pipe, not four.

TOP TIP! There are plenty of options for the goal net, but I found the cheapest and most readily available net to use was garden netting from the hardware store. A trailer cargo net is a stronger, but slightly more expensive, option as well.

THE PLAN

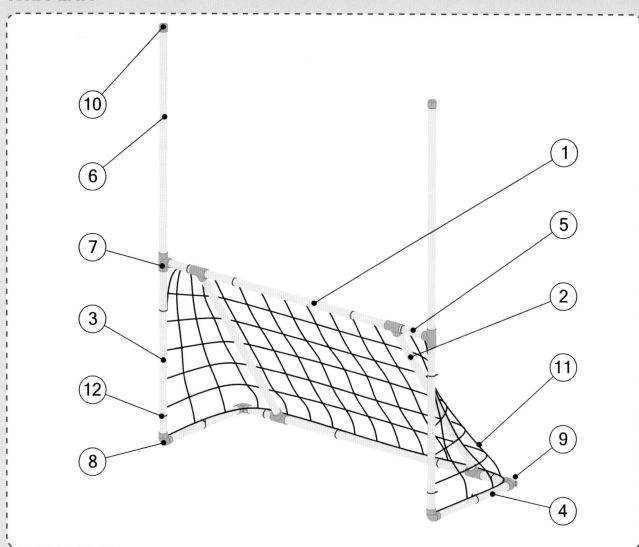

THE PARTS

Part	Description	Qty	Size	Material
1	Centre Beam	2	Ø40 x 1200	PVC Pipe
2	Brace Beam	2	Ø40 x 1100	PVC Pipe
3	Upright	2	Ø40 x 900	PVC Pipe
4	Side Beam	2	Ø40 x 600	PVC Pipe
5	End Beam	4	Ø40 x 200	PVC Pipe
6	Upright Extension	2	Ø40 x 1200	PVC Pipe
7	Tee	6	40mm	PVC
8	Elbow	2	40mm	PVC
9	Inspection Elbow	2	40mm	PVC
10	End Cap	2	40mm	PVC
11	Net	1	2.4m x 1.2m	
12	Cable Tie	14	200mm	

You can use these steps to construct a soccer goal, or a combination soccer/football goal by adding two upright extension posts.

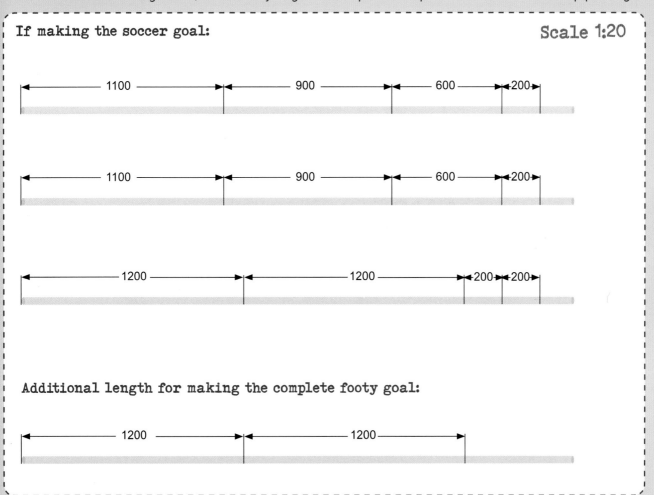

CUTTING GUIDE

Follow the below cutting order, to ensure you get all the pieces required out of the 3m PVC pipe lengths.

If making the soccer goal: Scale 1:20

|← 1100 →|← 900 →|← 600 →|←200→|

|← 1100 →|← 900 →|← 600 →|←200→|

|← 1200 →|← 1200 →|←200→|←200→|

Additional length for making the complete footy goal:

|← 1200 →|← 1200 →|

INSTRUCTIONS

Step 1

a. Make sure you have a large, clean, flat area to lay out all of the components during construction.

b. Measure and cut all the pipe lengths to size.

Step 2

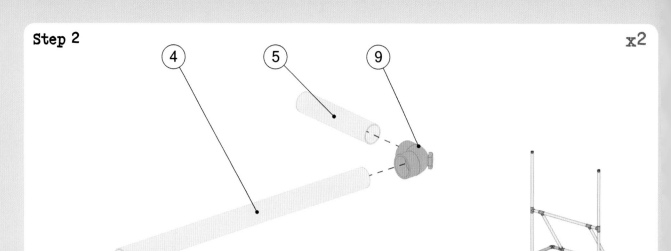

a. Glue the two base corners together. These corners use an inspection cap that will be required later.

TOP TIP! Always follow the manufacturer's instructions when using PVC cement, and only apply when you are certain the parts will align and fit—once glued they cannot be undone!

Step 3 (for footy goal)   x2

a. Glue the front corner sections together, using a tee piece at the intersection. These will be used to attach the goal uprights in Step 9.

Alternate Step 3 (for soccer goal)   x2

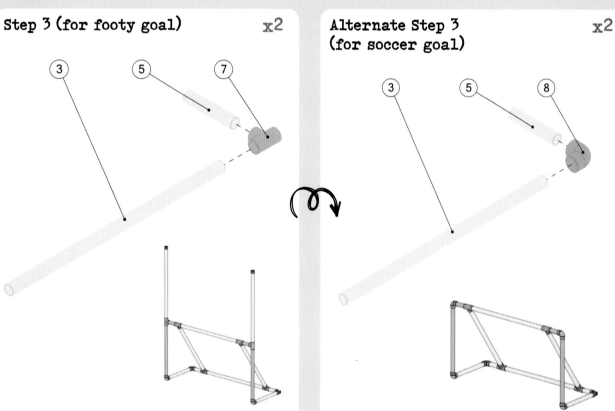

a. If you would prefer to make a soccer goal only, replace the two tees at the top of the front section with two elbow pieces.

Step 4

a. Put the assembled corner sections together to make the left and right ends. Note the corners are reversed on each end so they both face inwards to the goal.

TOP TIP! When aligning the pipes, push them into a floor/wall corner to help keep angles at 90 degrees.

Step 5

x2

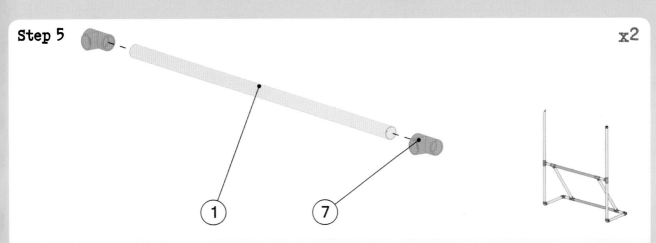

a. Glue the two centre beams to the tees, ensuring both tee pieces are flat. Any small angle will be exaggerated when the brace beams are added.

Step 6

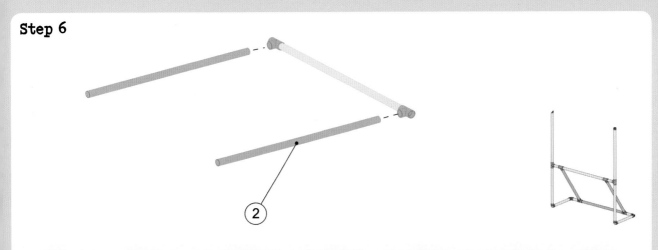

a. Glue the brace beams into one centre beam section only. Do not attach the second centre beam section until fully assembling the frame. (Complete this assembly in Step 7 when connecting the tee pieces to help keep all parts flat.)

Step 7

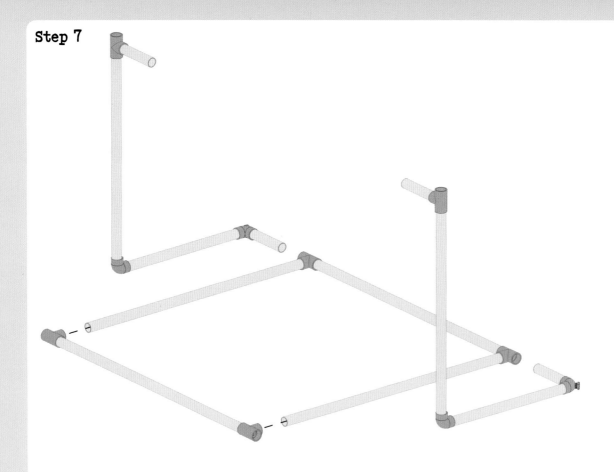

a. Lay all the pre-assembled pieces out on the floor.

b. Assemble without glue to check that everything fits, and then pull apart.

Step 8

a. Add glue and assemble all of the components.

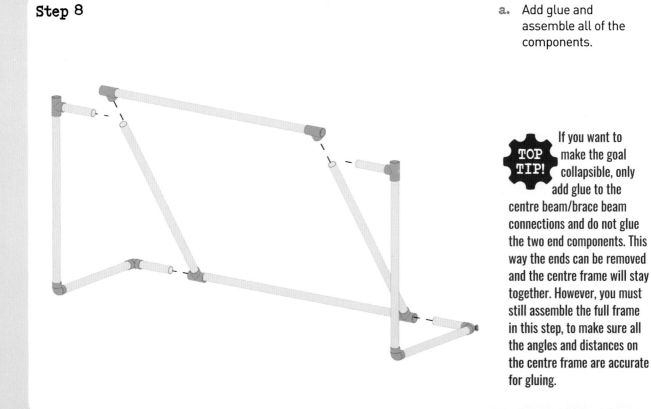

TOP TIP! If you want to make the goal collapsible, only add glue to the centre beam/brace beam connections and do not glue the two end components. This way the ends can be removed and the centre frame will stay together. However, you must still assemble the full frame in this step, to make sure all the angles and distances on the centre frame are accurate for gluing.

Step 9

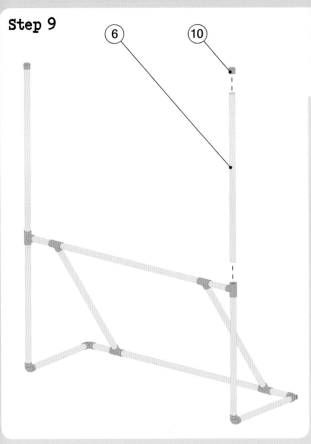

⑥ ⑩

a. Add the footy uprights and caps. If storage space is an issue, glue the end caps to the upright extension pieces, but don't glue the uprights to the goal. The uprights can then be removed to minimise space.

Step 10

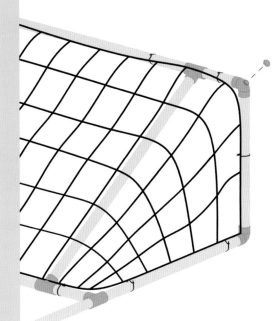

a. Add the net to the frame and cable tie in place. When attaching the cable ties, try to have them face away from accessible areas for safety. Once the net is securely attached, trim to size.

b. You can remove the inspection cap and fill the base with water to add weight and stability to the frame. If the ends are removable (not glued) they may not be water tight, so you can use sand to fill the base instead.

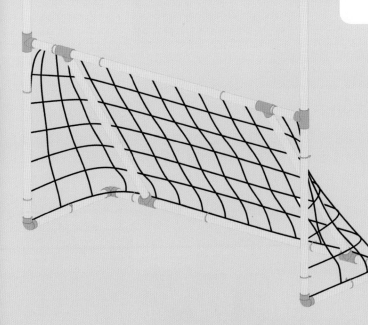

TENNIS BALL GAME

I don't know whether the kids or I have more fun with this one! This is either a game of random luck or one requiring extreme dexterity and accuracy—you decide! After a Saturday afternoon BBQ at my place, I have spent many quality—and very funny—hours playing this in the backyard with adults and kids alike.

The game is easy to play: you basically swing the tennis balls, connected by a rope, and release towards the frame. The momentum of the balls will wrap the rope around one of the three rungs. The bottom rung scores one point, the middle rung scores two points, and the top (and seemingly the toughest rung to wrap around) scores three points. Each player throws alternately, there are three shots each per round. First person to twenty-one wins. Pretty simple really and just as easy to put together.

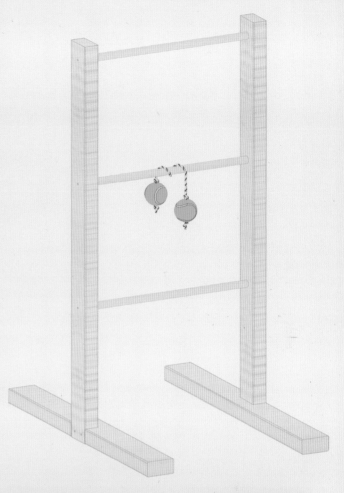

TOOL BOX

25mm chisel	Hammer	PVA glue
Drill	Handsaw	Screwdriver bit
Drill bits: 3mm, 5mm and 25mm spade bit	Pencil	Tape measure

SHOPPING LIST

Description	Qty	Size	Material
Skids	1	70 x 35 x 1200	Pine
Uprights	1	70 x 35 x 2000	Pine
Rails	1	Ø25 x 1800	Dowel
Treated Pine Screw	4	8g x 60	Galvanised
Treated Pine Screw	6	8g x 40	Galvanised
Tennis Balls	8		
Rope	1	6mm x 2.4m	

THE PLAN

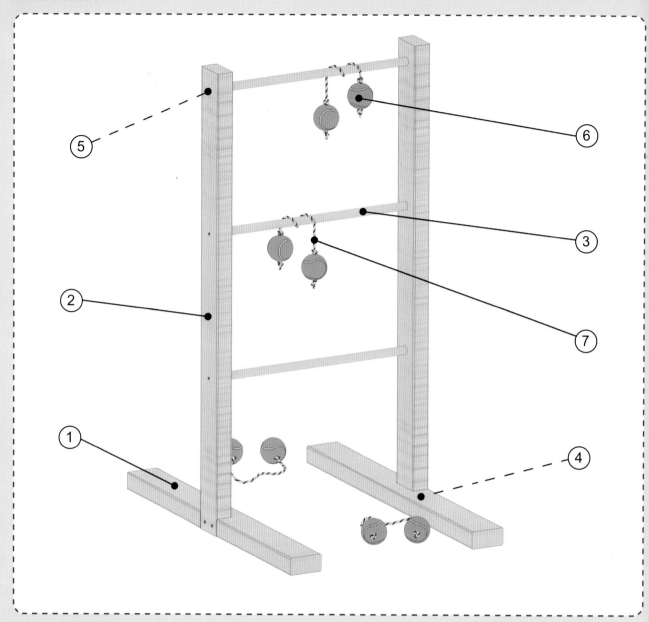

THE PARTS

Part	Description	Qty	Size	Material
1	Skid	2	70 x 35 x 600	Pine
2	Upright	2	70 x 35 x 1000	Pine
3	Rail	3	Ø25 x 600	Dowel
4	Treated Pine Screw	4	8g x 60	Galvanised
5	Treated Pine Screw	6	8g x 40	Galvanised
6	Tennis Ball	8		
7	Rope	4	6mm x 600mm	

INSTRUCTIONS

Step 1

x2

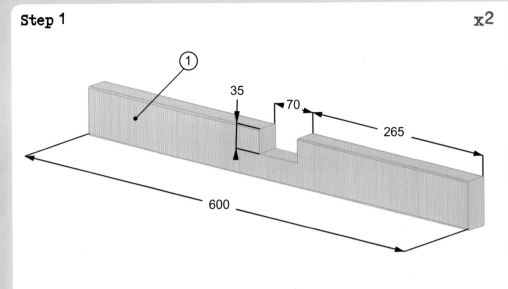

a. Cut the two skids to size.

b. Mark out and cut a housing joint halfway along each skid.

c. The size of the housing should be the same size as the timber for the uprights (70 x 35).

Step 2

x2

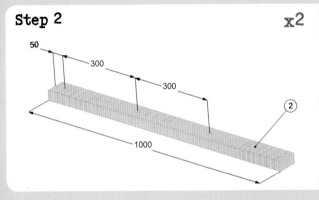

a. Cut the two uprights to size.

b. Mark out the spacing of the rails on both uprights, as shown in the diagram.

c. Using a 25mm spade bit, pre-drill three housing holes in each upright for the dowel rails. Drill until just the tip of the spade bit appears through the other side. This ensures each hole is the same depth and also shows an exact location for pre-drilling a pilot hole in the dowel rail once assembled.

Step 3

x2

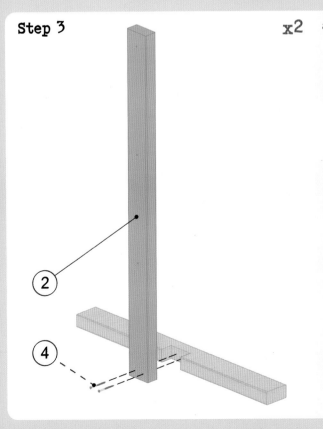

a. Glue and screw the upright to the skid, making sure to position the screws evenly and pre-drill through both pieces of timber. It is helpful to check the frame is square after putting in one screw. Adjustments can be easily made before fixing the second screw.

b. Repeat to attach the other upright. Remember to spin this second skid around, so you will have a left side and a right side. The holes in the uprights for the dowel should be facing each other.

TOP TIP! Pine is not a great external timber, unless it's coated. To avoid rot at the joins, smear the glue all over the timber concealed by the join before screwing. The glue will also act as a sealer.

Step 4

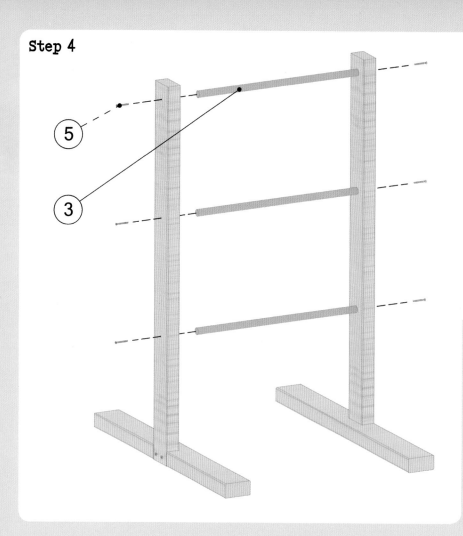

a. It's easier to paint each piece separately, so paint everything before you assemble.

b. Insert the rails into the pre-drilled housing holes on the uprights.

c. To prevent splitting, drill pilot holes into the dowel rails for the screws.

d. Screw the uprights to the dowel rails.

TOP TIP! Painting the rails different colours will help younger players with targeting and scoring.

If you insert screws in the ends of the rails, it will give you something to hold onto when painting the dowel—just remember to drill pilot holes first.

Step 5   x4

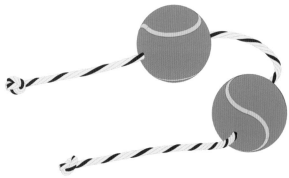

a. Cut the rope to four 600mm lengths. This is the best length to work with the spacing of the rails. Burn the ends of the ropes to prevent untwining.

b. Drill a hole for the rope on either side of each tennis ball.

c. Feed a rope through the holes of two tennis balls and position the tennis balls so they are spaced approximately the same distance apart as the rails. Tie a knot in both ends of the rope and trim any excess.

Step 6   x4

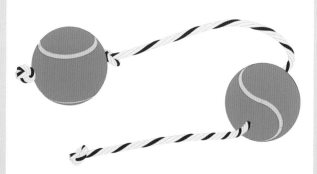

a. Move the tennis balls to the ends of the rope.

b. Tie a loose knot behind the tennis ball and slowly work the knot down the rope to tighten, locking the tennis ball in place.

TOP TIP! Use an old coathanger, or 1.5mm garden wire, with a small loop twisted at the end like a needle to feed the rope through both tennis ball holes, as you would with a needle and thread. Try finding different colour tennis balls for each set!

SWING

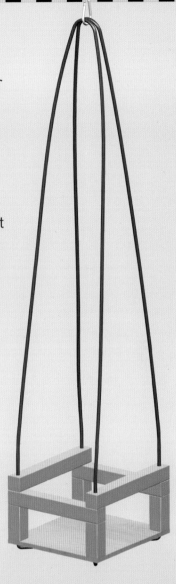

This is perhaps the best gift Grandpa ever came up with, and not least of all because he gave it to me twice. As a one year old I had plenty of fun swinging in it suspended from the family's pergola out the back. My brother and sister had their fair share of the action too.

Then it disappeared for a long time. We didn't think too much about it—we'd outgrown it eventually and moved on, occasionally reminiscing about it while flicking through old family photo albums. Anyway, once Gwenllian and I had our first child, Gruffydd, Grandpa obviously remembered it. He gave it a little TLC, a sand and a couple of coats of finish, and re-gifted it to me to be passed to my son on his first birthday. Thank you Theo Taylor, a family heirloom had been born.

SAFETY TIPS! This swing is best suited to children aged 1–3 years old. Children should never be left unattended when using the swing.

TOOL BOX

Circular saw or drop saw (ideal, but not essential)	**Duct tape**	**Pencil**
	Handsaw	**Tape measure**
Drill	**Palm sander** with 80	
Drill bits: 6mm and 12mm	and 120 grit sandpaper	

SHOPPING LIST

Description	Qty	Size	Material
Frame	1	42 x 42 x 1800	Pine
Base	1	350 x 320 x 12	Plywood
Rope	1	10mm x 7.5m	High-Strength Rope
Snap Hook	1	8mm	Stainless Steel

THE PLAN

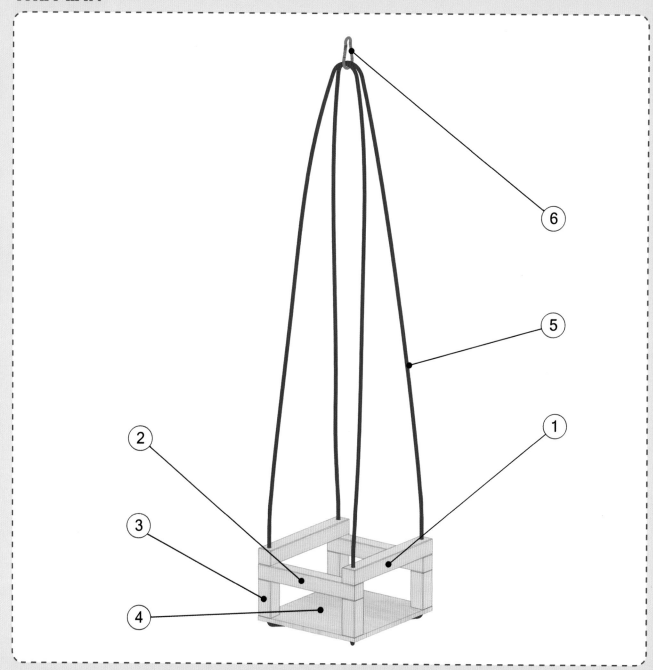

THE PARTS

Part	Description	Qty	Size	Material
1	Front	2	42 x 42 x 350	Pine
2	Side	2	42 x 42 x 320	Pine
3	Upright	4	42 x 42 x 100	Pine
4	Base	1	350 x 320 x 12	Plywood
5	Rope	1	10mm x 7.5m	High-Strength Rope
6	Snap Hook	1	8mm	Stainless Steel

Step 1

a. Measure and cut all the required pieces to size.

b. Sand the edges of all the timber pieces to have a slight round, in order to avoid any sharp edges or corners.

TOP TIP! Before drilling the 12mm holes in these steps, drill 6mm holes first—it's easier to ensure the bit stays centred and straight. Drilling with a 12mm bit requires a firm grip on the drill and clamping of the timber, because of the substantial amount of timber that is being dug out by the bit so quickly.

Step 2

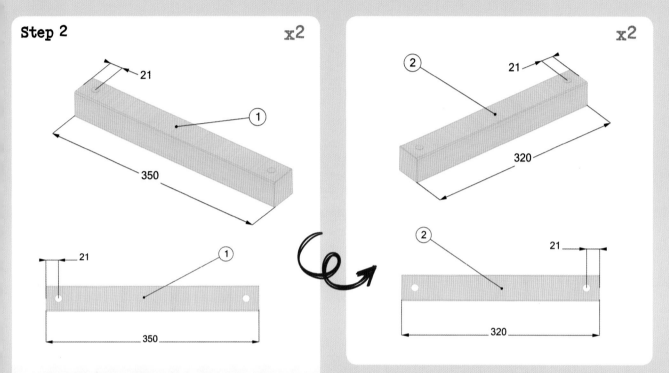

a. Mark out the positions of the holes for the rope in both front pieces.

b. Drill 12mm holes for the 10mm rope—you want to make the holes slightly larger than the rope, but not too much.

c. Repeat the above steps for the two side pieces.

TOP TIP! The position of the holes needs to be in the centre of the timber, from the end and sides. If you choose to use slightly larger or smaller timber than shown here, you will need to adjust your measurements accordingly.

Step 3

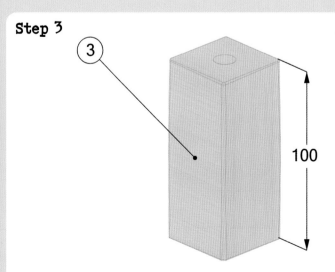

x4

a. Drill a 12mm hole through each of the uprights. Keep the drill straight and drill from the centre of both ends to make a straighter hole. Drilling into the end grain can be difficult, so use a clamp or bench vice to hold the timber firmly. (Don't worry if you are slightly off with your drilling. All parts of the swing move around quite freely once you are done, so minor imperfections won't be noticed.)

Step 4

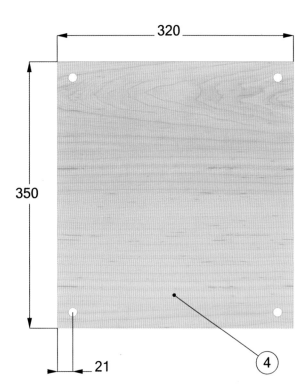

320

350

21

4

a. Drill the same size holes in each corner of the base.

TOP TIP! The longer rails go on the top of the side pieces, and will be the front and back of the seat, to allow a little more space for the legs.

Step 5

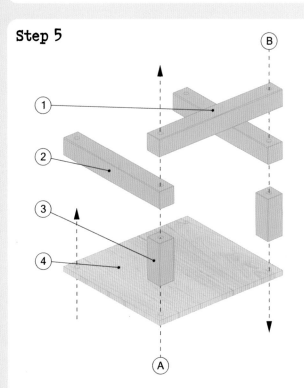

B

1

2

3

4

A

a. Start to assemble the swing.

b. Feed the rope through the holes, starting from underneath the base.

c. Follow the direction indicated in the diagram: up through Ⓐ, across to Ⓑ and down to underneath the base again. (The length of the swing's ropes will be able to be adjusted evenly once all the components are assembled and tied off.)

Step 6

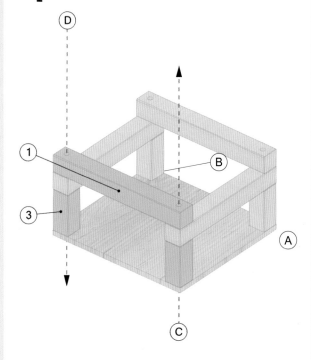

D

1

B

3

A

C

a. Under the base, cross the rope diagonally from corner Ⓑ to corner Ⓒ. Position the rest of the pieces and continue to push the rope through the holes.

b. Feed the rope up through Ⓒ and down through Ⓓ.

Step 7

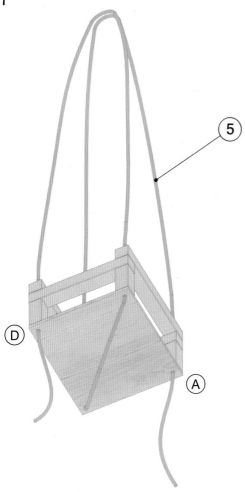

a. You will now have two loose ends under the base, diagonally opposite each other at corners Ⓐ and Ⓓ.

Step 8

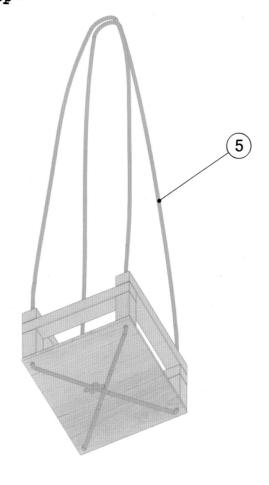

a. Pull the rope through to tie the knot then pull tight and adjust so the swing hangs evenly when suspended.

Step 9

a. Use a good quality, strong stainless steel snap hook to clip around the rope at the top of the swing.

b. Once the swing is hanging flat and even, you can bind the ropes at the top with some duct tape to prevent them sliding out of position.

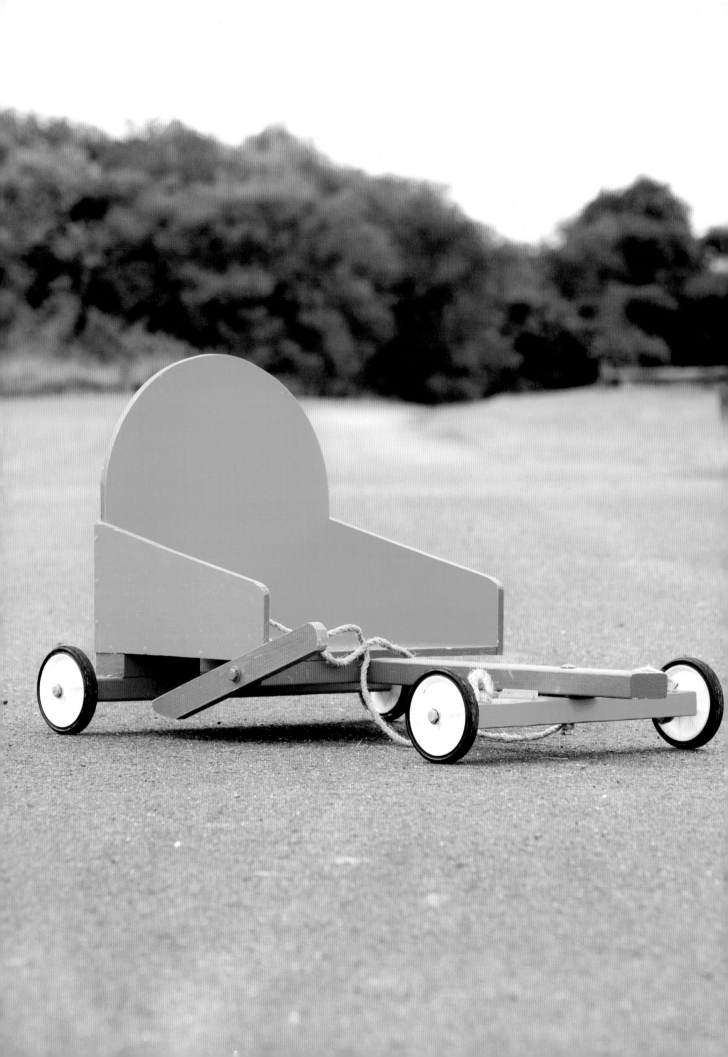

BILLY CART

I've lost count on how many times, as a kid, I attached wheels to something and sent it downhill, manned and shrieking with excitement as it went. The imagination of the young may be extraordinary in its wonder, though it is not always the most reliable of blueprints when it comes to billy carts. This one is a fairly simple and easily constructed version that will get you on your way without getting too technical. It will have the kids tearing around the parkland like there is no tomorrow. It's a reliable seat on four wheels with a rope for steering and a brake for the nervous amongst riders.

SAFETY TIPS! Always wear a helmet and safety pads, and never ride on the road. This billy cart is intended for use by kids up to 35kgs. To ensure the safety of bigger kids, add a metal strap around the axle to prevent the pressure from the coach bolt splitting the timber. It's a good idea to check the tightness of the coach bolts in the wheels before each use.

TOOL BOX

Circular saw (ideal, but not essential)	**Handsaw**	**Straight edge**
	Multigrips	**Tape measure**
Drill	**Pencil**	
Drill bits: 3mm, 5mm and 10mm	**Shifter and socket spanner**	

SHOPPING LIST

Description	Qty	Size	Material
Frame	3	70 x 35 x 1200	Pine
Seat	1	1200 x 600 x 12	Plywood
Brake	1	35 x 35 x 400	Pine
Foot Guides	1	19 x 19 x 280	Pine Tri Quad
Treated Pine Screw	27	8g x 38	Galvanised
Treated Pine Screw	6	8g x 60	Galvanised
Coach Screw	5	10mm x 75	Galvanised
Cup Head Bolt	2	12mm x 100	Galvanised
Washer	10	10mm	Galvanised
Washer	3	12mm	Galvanised
Nut	3	M12	Galvanised
Nail	8	30 x 2.0	Galvanised
Wheel	4	150mm	
High-Strength Rope	1	10mm x 3m	

THE PLAN

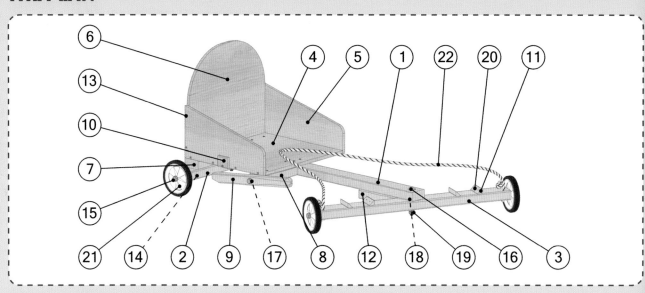

THE PARTS

Part	Description	Qty	Size	Material
1	Centre Beam	1	70 x 35 x 1000	Pine
2	Rear Axle	1	70 x 35 x 600	Pine
3	Front Axle	1	70 x 35 x 800	Pine
4	Seat	1	400 x 440 x 12	Plywood
5	Side	2	412 x 200 x 12	Plywood
6	Seat Back	1	400 x 440 x 12	Plywood
7	Seat Support	2	70 x 35 x 150	Pine
8	Brake Support	1	70 x 35 x 200	Pine
9	Brake	1	35 x 35 x 400	Pine
10	Brake Stop	1	42 x 50 x 12	Plywood
11	Foot Guide	4	19 x 19 x 70	Pine Tri Quad
12	Oversteer Block	1	70 x 35 x 200	Pine
13	Treated Pine Screw	27	8g x 38	Galvanised
14	Treated Pine Screw	6	8g x 60	Galvanised
15	Coach Screw	5	10mm x 75	Galvanised
16	Cup Head Bolt	2	12mm x 100	Galvanised
17	Washer	10	10mm	Galvanised
18	Washer	3	12mm	Galvanised
19	Nut	3	M12	Galvanised
20	Nail	8	30 x 2.0	Galvanised
21	Wheel	4	150mm	
22	High-Strength Rope	1	10mm x 3m	

INSTRUCTIONS

Step 1

a. Measure and cut the frame pieces to size. Sand to clean up edges.

Step 2

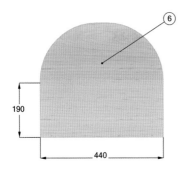

a. Cut the seat back to shape, as shown in the diagram. Sand to clean up edges.

b. Measure and mark out positions for the four screws along the bottom of the seat back, spacing evenly.

c. Drill clearance holes for the screws and countersink.

Step 3

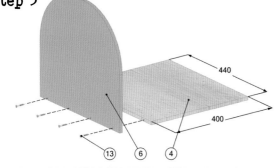

a. Measure and cut the seat panel to size. Sand to clean up edges.

b. Drill pilot holes for the screws into the seat panel to prevent splitting. (Make sure you drill into the long-edge of the base panel.)

c. Screw the seat back to the seat.

Step 4

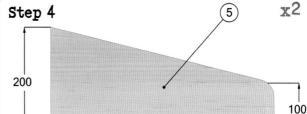

x2

a. Cut the side pieces of the seat and sand edges.

b. Mark out the screw holes and pre-drill clearance holes and countersink as before in Step 2.

Step 5

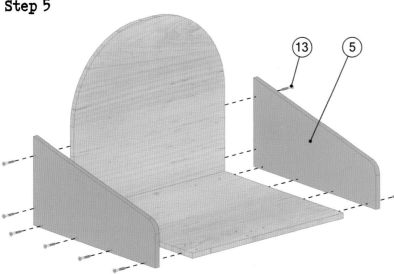

TOP TIP!

I usually put my first screw about 50mm (or at least the length of the screw I'm using) in from the end of the timber. That way I'm sure not to have screws coming in from different sides hitting each other and ruining the job. Plus, the material you are screwing into is less likely to split.

a. Drill pilot holes for the screws into both short sides of the seat panel to prevent splitting.

b. Add the two sides to finish the seat.

Step 6

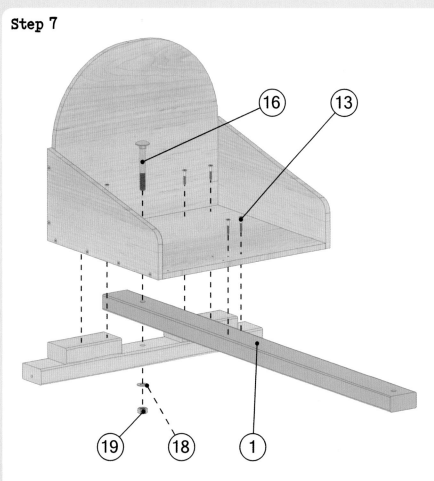

a. Screw the two seat supports to the axle beam, 68mm from each end.

Step 7

a. Align the seat, rear axle beam and centre beam in position to check that they fit properly. The axle beam will protrude 100mm from the back face of the seat—this prevents the cart from tipping on its back.

b. Screw the seat to the seat supports and beam. Pre-drill for the screws, allowing enough room so that the drill/driver doesn't foul on the seat back as the screws are driven. Use six screws as shown in the diagram.

c. Locate the centre beam in position.

d. While all in position, drill a hole for the bolt through the seat, centre beam and axle beam, and fit the bolt. Be sure to add the washer between the nut and the timber. Add the washer, nut and a locking nut to prevent the bolt working loose.

 Be sure to countersink any holes in the seat so no screws are sticking up.

Step 8

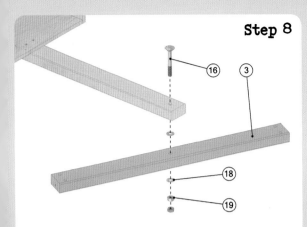

a. Drill a hole in the centre of the front axle.

b. Check the length of the centre beam. You may need to shorten it so that the driver's legs can comfortably reach the front axle in its final position.

c. Drill a hole in the centre beam, 35mm from the end, for attaching the axle. (You could also drill another hole further down the axle to reposition for shorter drivers. This would only require moving one bolt.)

d. Bolt the centre beam to the front axle, making sure to add the washer in between the two pieces of timber.

e. Using two nuts under the axle allows you to tighten one against the other so they won't work loose as the axle repeatedly turns. The second nut is referred to as a locking nut.

Step 9

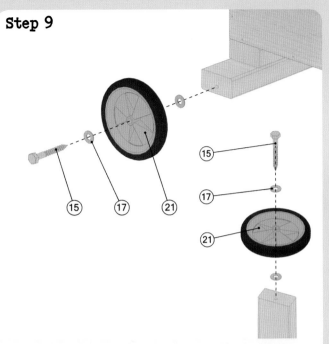

a. There are plenty of ways to attach wheels, but I found that this was an inexpensive and simple process. And plenty strong enough for little tackers!

b. Pre-drill pilot holes in both ends of the front and rear axle beams for the coach bolt for the wheels. (See TIPS AND TECHNIQUES for more on drilling into end grain.) Position the pilot holes around 5mm below the centre of the axle. It is best to have plenty of timber above the bolt for strength.

c. Check the inside diameter of the hole in the wheels and change the size of the coach screws if needed. The screw should be a snug fit in the wheel.

d. Tighten the screw then back it off half a turn. You need the wheel to spin, but too much sideways movement is not good either.

Step 10

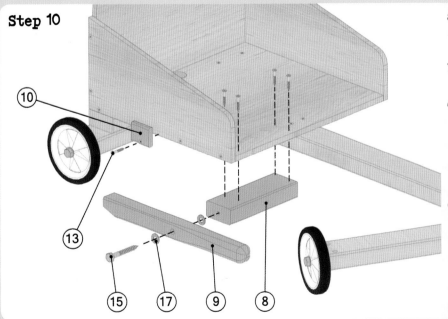

a. Sand the edges of the brake handle to shape for hand comfort.

b. Drill a hole in the centre of the brake handle piece.

c. Attach the brake support. Screw to the seat first, and then add the brake handle by following the same instructions for attaching the wheels in Step 9.

d. Use an offcut of the plywood to cut a small brake stop, and screw to the seat above the brake handle. This will prevent the handle dropping forward.

Step 11

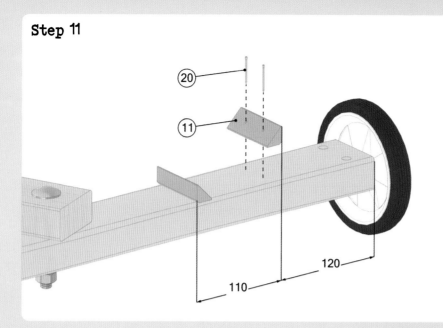

(20)

(11)

120

110

a. Glue and nail four pieces of tri-quad moulding to the top of the front axle, evenly spaced from the centre. These will allow the driver's feet to rest in a good spot for steady and even turning.

Step 12

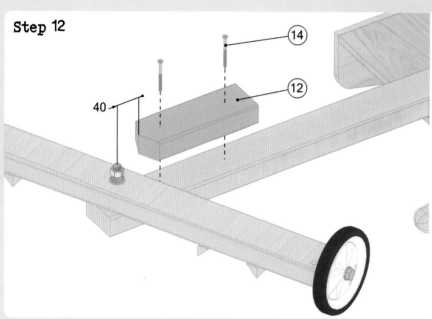

(14)

(12)

40

a. Turn the billy cart over and screw the oversteer block to the underside of the centre beam. This will act as a safety feature to stop the axle from over-turning. You can adjust the position of the block to change this oversteer restriction, so the cart turns as sharply or as gently as you like. I'd recommend a gentle turn to start with.

Step 13

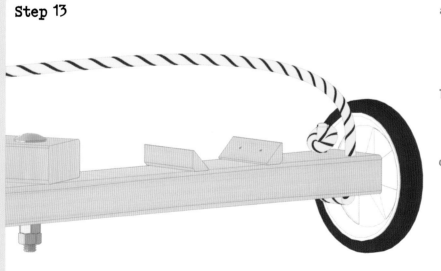

a. Drill two holes through the front axle at both ends. Make sure you drill either side of the coach screw so you don't hit it.

b. Feed the rope down through the front hole then back up through the back hole before tying off in a knot.

c. Repeat on the other side with the other end of the rope. Check the rope length is suitable for the driver, and shorten if needed before tying the second knot.

RAINY DAY ACTIVITIES

DRAGON SHELF

I reckon that the way something is presented has a lot to do with the enthusiasm that a child will have for it. Just have a go at the nutso stuff we parents sometimes do to veggies to get the desired result. (Yep, I too am guilty of making a face out of veg, and begging my young bloke not to devour it . . . got him, yes!)

How about dressing up books to make the thought of them even more exciting, and their home an imagination wonderland for your kids?

And if you want to spread your creative wings for this one, then go for it! An animal like an elephant could work pretty well too I think. Or you can just copy mine (which actually has its own wings—dragon wings!) by following the included cutting guide.

A friendly dragon in the bedroom to look after and display your child's books and treasures is great way to ensure that the light of creative play and imagination remains bright at your place. The kids will be pretty chuffed with your DIY skills too.

TOOL BOX

Chalk line (helpful, but not essential)
Circular saw (optional)
Clamps
Drill
Drill bits: 3mm and 5mm plus
  screwdriver bits
Jigsaw plus timber scrolling blade,
  rough cut and fine cut blades
Masonry bits for fixing to masonry
  walls (if required)
Pencil
PVA glue
Screwdriver
Straight edge
Tape measure

SHOPPING LIST

Description	Qty	Size	Material
Timber	1	2400 x 1200 x 15	Plywood
Treated Pine Screw	36	8g x 45	

THE PLAN

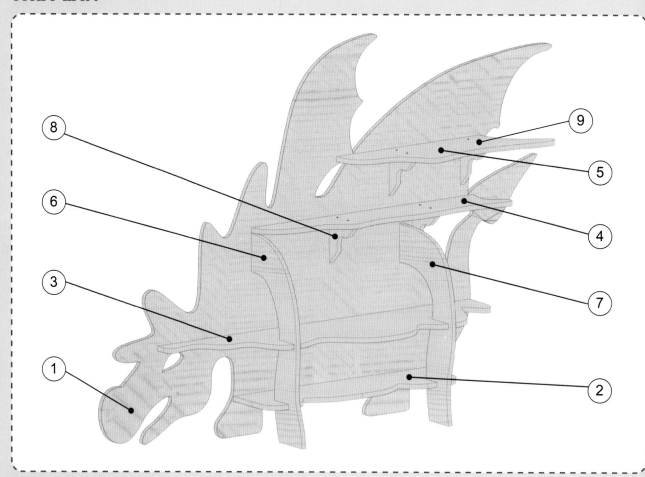

THE PARTS

Part	Description	Qty	Size	Material
1	Back	1	1800 x 1200 x 15	Plywood
2	Shelf 1	1	740 x 200 x 15	Plywood
3	Shelf 2	1	1200 x 300 x 15	Plywood
4	Shelf 3	1	900 x 150 x 15	Plywood
5	Shelf 4	1	700 x 200 x 15	Plywood
6	Left Leg	1	620 x 270 x 15	Plywood
7	Right Leg	1	580 x 280 x 15	Plywood
8	Bracket	4	130 x 130 x 15	Plywood
9	Treated Pine Screw	36	8g x 45	

CUTTING GUIDE

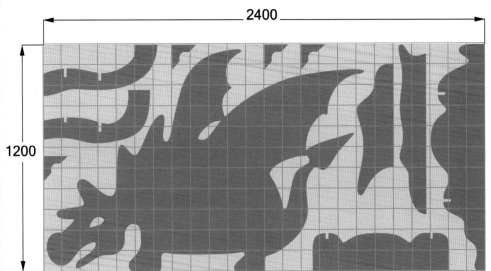

2400

1200

Scale 1:20

A grid will help get the design and sizing bang on! Measure 100mm intervals along opposite sides starting at the same end. And then use a chalk line and reel to snap the lines across the board.

a. Draw a 100mm grid on the sheet of plywood and mark out all of the shapes, as per the design above.

b. Be sure to follow the measuring up guide on page 110 for exact measurements for the shelves—they are crucial for being able to slot these parts of the frame together.

c. The curves are a little less critical and you can modify the decorative shape if preferred. Just check the shelf positions first, and ensure they pass through where the wings and tail overlap.

CUTTING ORDER

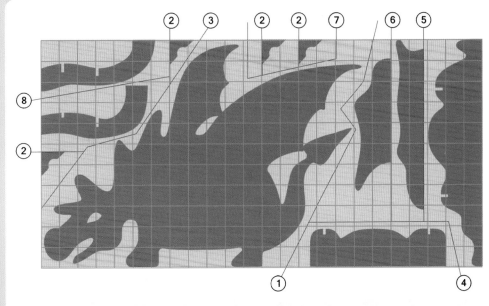

TOP TIP! Place timbers under the board at each end and either side of the cut to elevate and support each piece. Check that it is high enough for the saw blade to miss the bench. When clamping off the edge of a bench for jigsawing, keep the cut close to the bench edge to reduce the bouncing vibration of the timber.

a. Cut the pieces in the order shown to help make handling easier.

b. Use a straight-edge guide for cuts ②, ⑤ and ⑥. Separating the larger piece into smaller pieces will make them easier to handle and allow the curves to be cut more accurately.

c. When making cuts ②, be careful not to go beyond the red line indicated and cut into the other pieces. Use a scrolling blade on the jigsaw and cut right to the line. Small pieces are harder to hold and trim with a saw later. For the larger pieces it is far easier to cut wide of the line quickly and then move and clamp each piece as you cut out the detail. See TIPS AND TECHNIQUES for more tips on cutting.

d. Remember to double check the sizes and positions of the shelf slots on the measuring up guide before cutting them out.

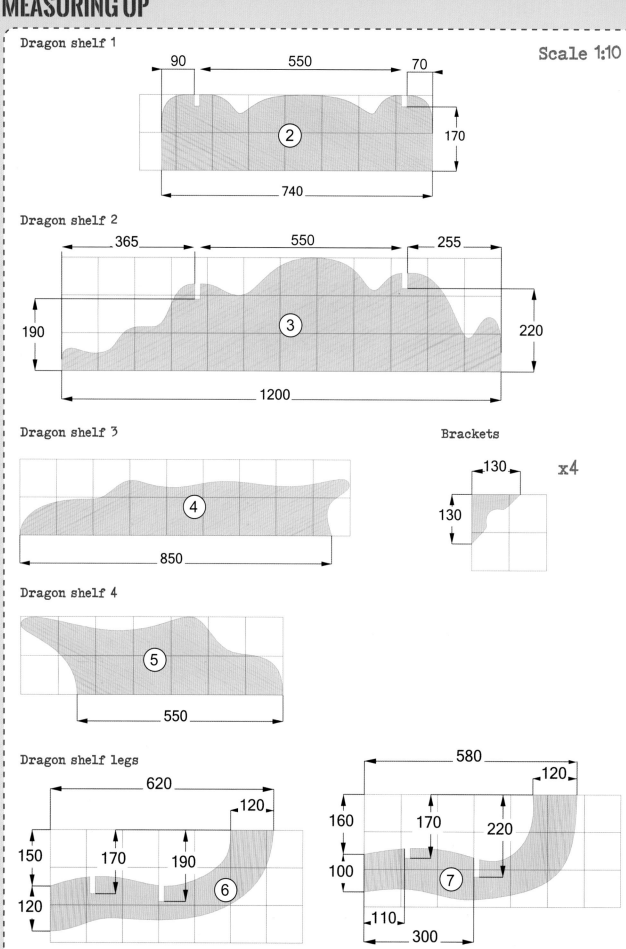

Dragon shelf 1

Scale 1:10

Dragon shelf 2

Dragon shelf 3

Brackets

x4

Dragon shelf 4

Dragon shelf legs

INSTRUCTIONS

Step 1

a. Follow the cutting and measuring up guides to cut out all the pieces. Sand to clean edges.

b. For this project, I did a complete dry fit—which means joining everything without glue first, then taking apart completely to paint. Re-assembly is dead easy once all your screw holes have been established.

Step 2

a. Assemble the legs and the two lower shelves.

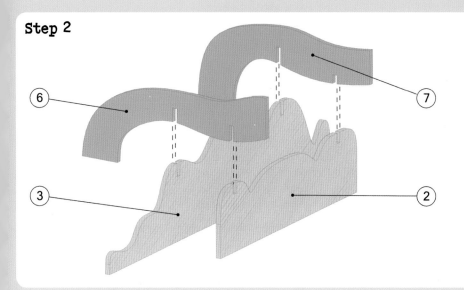

Step 3

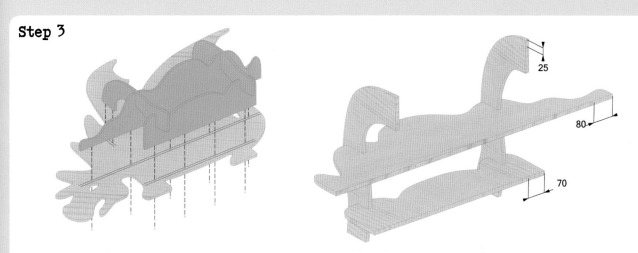

a. All the screws for the shelves should be from the back side of the dragon. Position the legs and shelves in place on the dragon to check. Once in the correct position, mark the location of the boards on the back piece.

b. Remove the legs and shelves from the dragon body and drill clearance holes for the screws in the desired locations.

c. Reposition the legs and shelves and drill the pilot holes back through the legs and shelves from the back side of the dragon.

d. Screw the legs and shelves to the back piece.

TOP TIP! Make sure that all four flat edges in the shelving unit hit the dragon together. I attached the pieces with the dragon lying down on two saw horses—it made it easy to use a square at the same time as screwing up from underneath. Gravity is sometimes a great assistant!

Step 4

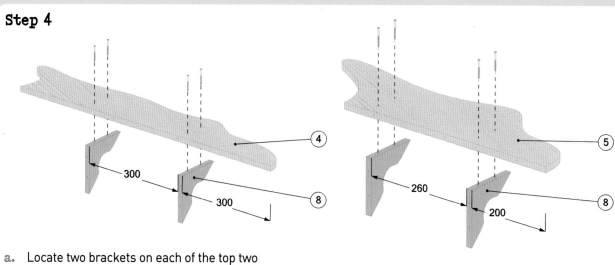

a. Locate two brackets on each of the top two shelves. Double check that the angle of your brackets are 90 degrees in order to make sure that your shelves will sit square off the dragon.

b. Mark and drill clearance and pilot holes, ensuring the screws are not too close to the narrow end of the bracket, so they don't protrude through.

c. Ensure the back of the shelf and the brackets are flush with each other.

Step 5

a. Refer to the diagram to mark out the shelf heights for the top two shelves.

b. Once the shelves are in position, drill pilot and clearance holes, as in Step 3.

c. Screw the shelves on to the back piece.

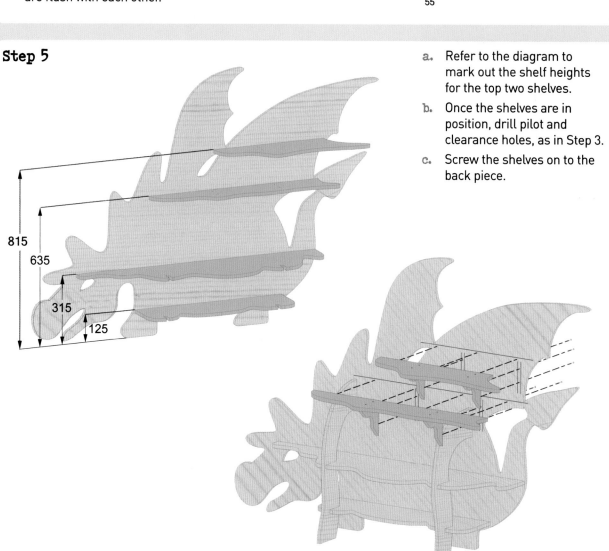

NOW FOR PAINTING!

Step 6

a. It may seem like you are undoing your work, but painting the pieces separately while lying flat is far easier and faster, and will give you a first-class finish.

b. I rolled the whole job with a primer and then three coats of enamel on both sides. There is a longer drying time between coats of enamel paint than acrylic—being patient and using less paint for each coat, but applying more coats, will give a more consistent build-up of paint for a better finish.

TO ATTACH TO THE WALL ...

All bookcases, friendly fire-breathing ones included, should be attached to the wall to prevent toppling.

For blockwork, brick or masonry: Drill a clearance hole above the top shelf, somewhere near the centre of the bookcase, insert a plug in the masonry behind and attach the shelving.

For plasterboard walls: Locate a timber framing stud as near to the centre of the bookcase as possible, drill a clearance hole in the dragon and drive a screw directly into the timber stud behind. Consider attaching with two screws to give each screw a little support.

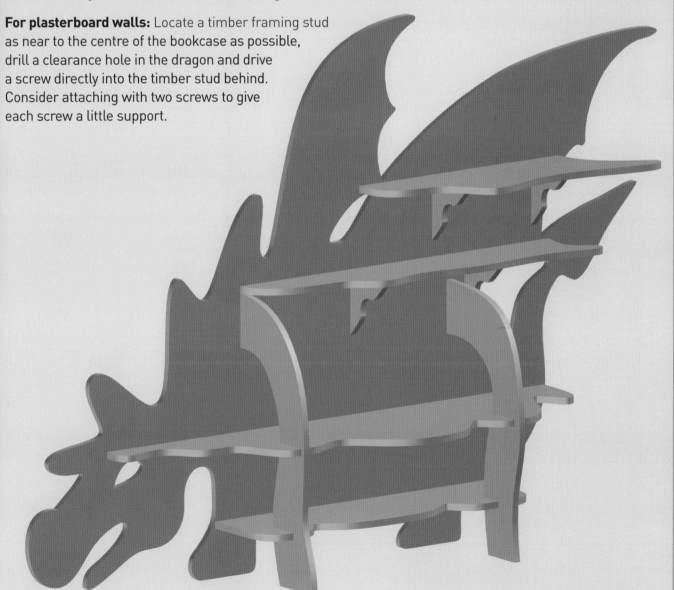

FAIRY HOUSE

This fairly simple project is still absorbing my eight-year-old daughter, Branwen's, attention a good three years after it was made for her, and has now also captured the attention of our two-year-old, Greta. The mystery and fantasy that goes along with something so organic and natural is hard to grow out of.

We were on a weekend away at Kangaroo Valley in NSW when I wandered into a timber craft store. I'm a big fan of these shops; they are a great place for locals to express ideas and skills with timber that really hit the bullseye. For me, or more importantly, for Branwen, in this case it was a beautifully built home for fairies made out of a section of tree trunk. The price tag seemed worth it for the care and love that must've gone into it, but this was a project that I really wanted to have a crack at myself.

So when a garbage truck accidentally knocked down a large branch off a gumtree out the front of our house a year or so later, I knew there had to be a fairy house in there somewhere.

TOOL BOX

18mm chisel
Clamps
Drill
Drill bits:
   12mm speedbor bit
   and countersink bit
Hammer (preferably a
   lump hammer)
Handsaw

Holesaw or spade bits in
   various sizes
Jigsaw
Pencil
PVA glue
Rotary tool (very helpful,
   but not essential)
Sandpaper coarse and fine

SHOPPING LIST

Description	Qty	Size	Material
Base	1	450 x 450 x 12	Plywood
Roof	2	90 x 9 x 150	Hardwood (offcut)
Nail	4	25 x 1.6	
Hinge	2	25mm	Brass
Wood Screw	4	6g x 25	
Wood Screw	8	To suit hinges	Brass

 TOP TIP! The shopping list and parts list for this project are meant as a rough guide only. This is more of a creative design, so follow the basic steps and equipment used, but all sizes and designs should be modified to suit the size and shape of the log you work with—and your own imagination!

THE PLAN

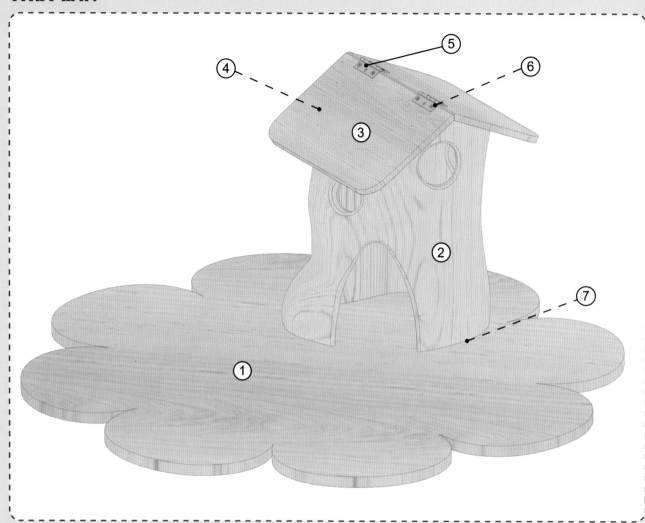

THE PARTS

Part	Description	Qty	Size	Material
1	Base	1	450 x 450 x 12	Plywood
2	Log	1	Approx. Ø120	
3	Roof	2	90 x 9 x 150	Hardwood
4	Nail	4	25 x 1.6	
5	Hinges	2	25mm	Brass
6	Wood Screws	4	6g x 25	
7	Wood Screws	8	To suit hinges	Brass

INSTRUCTIONS

Step 1

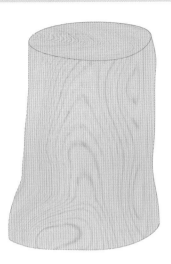

a. Find a suitable log and clean it up. A small section of tree works best—I used part of a branch with a fork in it, about 220mm tall. Cutting a section through a fork in the branch will give a wider, more stable base.

b. Remove any loose bark or timber, then cut the ends flat with a large handsaw.

c. Try to make the cuts close to square with the overall length of the branch. The less square the cut, the more the house will have a Leaning Tower of Pisa look.

Step 2

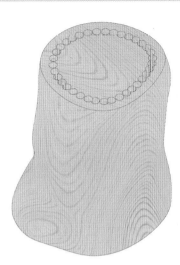

a. Use a speedbor bit to drill a series of holes around the inside circumference of the sap wood. You are essentially drilling a ring around the core of the log. It is important to drill leaving 10mm of timber over and above any thickness of bark that you have. The point of the speedbor bit will enable you to slightly overlap each hole with the next. You will need to drill in from either end until the holes meet in the centre.

 TOP TIP! I used a rotary tool with various attachments to clean up the inside of the log—it gives you a nice smooth finish. You could also try a wire brush attachment and/or a sanding drum on a cordless drill.

Step 3

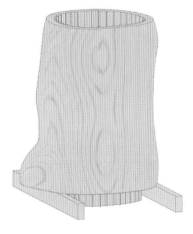

a. Sit the log on blocks, with as much of the edge as possible being supported.

b. Strike the centre of the wood solidly with a hammer to knock the core down and out of the middle. You may find more drilling is required, from either end.

c. Use chisels and a hammer, or a rotary tool, to tidy up the inside face of the log.

Step 4

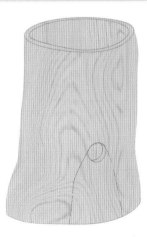

a. Think about where you would like to have the door and windows, and mark them roughly in location.

b. Start by drilling a hole for the top of the door. Always clamp the inside edge of the log at the point opposite where you are drilling or cutting.

Step 5

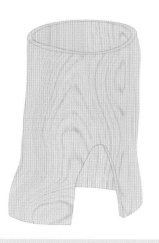

a. Use a jigsaw to carefully cut out the shape of the door.

Step 6

a. Next mark out the angles for the roof.

b. Prop the log and clamp it at an angle to enable a near-vertical cut.

c. Cut the angles. The safest way to make the cut is with a handsaw. Cutting vertically will make it neater and easier—you will be able to sight the cut as you make it and keep the handsaw blade straight.

d. To ensure both sides of the roof are in alignment, start the second cut from the apex (the top point) of the roof. Begin the second cut by lining the saw blade up with the two opposite points that mark the beginning of the previous cut.

e. After cutting, sand both sides flat if necessary.

Step 7

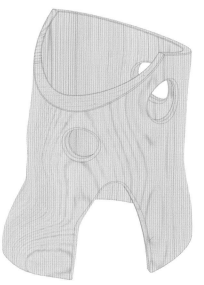

 TOP TIP! If a hinged, pitched roof with an apex seems too much, you could cut the one angle all the way through the log for a single-pitched, skillion-type roof that lays on top. Or you can just make a shallow cone out of cardboard, which will eliminate the roof pitch cut altogether.

a. Adjust the position of windows if required so they don't interfere with the roof and door.

b. Drill out the windows using various sized holesaws or speedbor bits.

c. Sand all edges around the door and windows.

Get help to sand the edges and prepare the house for the roof!

Step 7

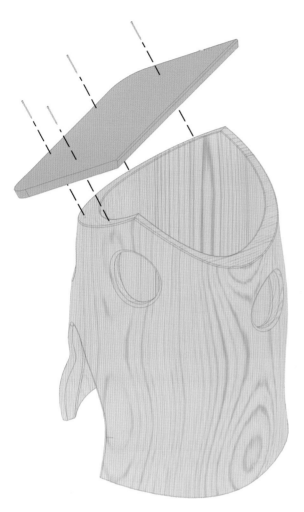

a. Cut two roof pieces to size and shape, allowing for any desired overhang.

b. Plane or sand the two top adjoining edges that meet at the apex of the roof so that when they are resting in position the edges are vertical and meet neatly. (In roofing terms, this is known as a plum cut.)

c. Fix one side of the roof to the log using glue and nails. Remember to drill 1mm pilot holes for the nails—even tiny pins can benefit from pilot holes.

Step 8

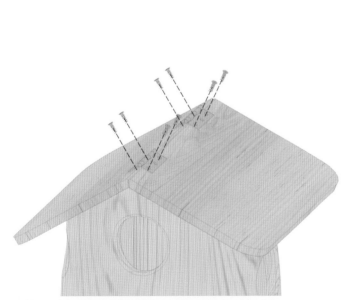

a. Position the second roof piece in place and mark the placement of the hinges on both sides.

b. Drill pilot holes and screw the hinges into both roof pieces.

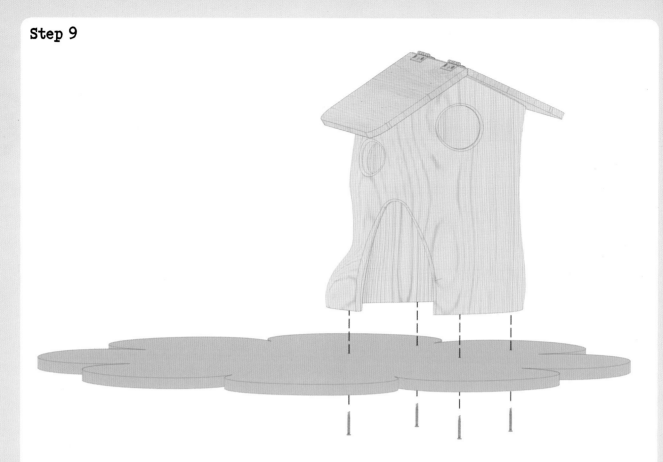

a. Make a base platform, cutting to whatever size and shape you desire.

b. Place the log somewhere off-centre on the base (a lot of play will be out the front of the house, so positioning to one side will give the fairies more garden to play with).

c. Trace the outline of the log onto the base. Remove the log and drill clearance holes in the base.

d. Put the log back in position and drill pilot holes into the log.

e. Apply PVA glue and screw the log to the base from underneath. Countersink the screw heads so they don't scratch any surface that the base is sitting on and add felt pads for extra protection.

TIME FOR DECORATING!

Decorate the fairy house with any little ornaments you can find. We headed down to the beach to find stuff like shells and pebbles. We also bought a couple of mushrooms and mini flowerpots from a craft store to sit by the fairy house front door. You could even cover the base with lawn before screwing the log house into position. A hot glue gun is perfect for instant bonds when securing all your shells and ornaments. Or you can combine drill holes with hot glue to stand up pointy objects.

TIPS & TECHNIQUES

TIPS &
TECHNIQUES

TIPS &
TECHNIQUES

TIPS &
TECHNIQUES

BENCH HOOK

A bench hook is absolutely essential for any hand cutting—with it, a steady grip from your hand and the force of the hand tool, combined with gravity mean that the piece you are cutting will stay in place. Bench hooks are dead simple to make and are best made up out of scrap material, so they are effectively free.

Get a piece of timber for the base (this can be any size you like, I find plywood a good material to use; somewhere around 300 x 300 x 12 should be about right). Attach a baton of timber flush to one end for the hook, flip the base over and attach another timber baton flush to the other end for the backstop. When screwing the pieces together keep in mind that it is stronger to screw through the thin ply into the thicker baton below.

You hold whatever you're cutting against the backstop and cut to one side of it so make sure the backstop is shorter than the base piece. You can set up bench hooks for right handers, left handers, or both.

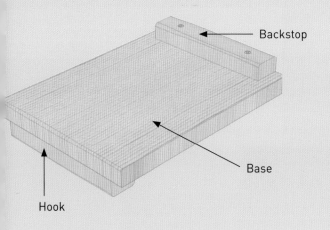

Backstop

Base

Hook

BENCH VICE

To make your own makeshift bench vice, clamp a block of timber to your bench then stand the piece you need to hold steady next to it, and clamp this to the timber block.

This will ensure the piece you are working on stands stable and you can use two hands to cut or drill more precisely.

CHISELLING

When working with a chisel in a housing, if the bevel of the chisel is facing up, the chisel tends to dig into the timber and can often take chunks out of the job, making it untidy. When the bevel is facing the job (the flat side of the chisel is facing up), you will need to lift the handle up to an angle similar to the angle of the bevel on the chisel. It may feel like you are going to dig the blade in deep, however the chisel will pair away the timber more neatly as you tap it with the hammer. By adjusting the angle slightly you can take more or less timber very neatly, and avoid unwanted digging in to the job.

CIRCULAR SAW STRAIGHT LINE CUTTING

Whenever you need to cut up sheet material into pieces with straight edges it is very helpful to use a straight edge that you can run the saw along to ensure the best possible finish.

While the saw is unplugged, measure from the edge of the saw plate to the far face of the saw blade and keep this measurement. (You can even put some masking tape on the saw with the number on it so you don't forget.) By adding this number to any size of piece you require, and clamping the straight edge in this position, you can easily run the saw plate along the straight edge so you are left with a perfectly straight piece at the size you're after. This will work when the straight edge is clamped to the waste piece.

If you are clamping your straight edge to the piece that you wish to keep, just measure from the saw plate to the near-side of the saw blade and subtract that measurement from the overall finished size you are after to get the position for your straight edge.

CLEARANCE HOLES

These should be drilled with a drill bit to make a hole the screw can pass through until it is caught by the screw head. The thread and shaft of the screw should pass right through. Basically, it is the head of the screw that holds one piece of timber against another, using the thread of the screw as an anchor.

COUNTERSINKING NAILS

If you are nailing into hardwood, or near the end of a piece of timber, the bullet head (fatter than the rest of the nail) can sometimes cause a split as it buries flush with the timber. A tip to avoid this late splitting is to turn the nail upside down before you drive it in and rest the bullet head in its final location. Hit the sharp end of the nail with your hammer. This creates a small indent, the same size as the nail head, before any pressure is put on the timber by the thickness of the nail. You can then drive the nail in as normal and as the head meets the surface of the job there is a space already there for it and the risk of splitting is greatly reduced.

COUNTERSINKING SCREWS

To allow the head of a screw to sit neatly flush with the surface, it is advised to drill a space with a countersinking bit. Some screws are self-countersinking (though even a screw with a self-countersinking head can cause splitting in small pieces of timber).

Many countersink bits have a tendency to leave a rough and uneven finish. A top tip to achieve a perfectly smooth countersink is to finish every countersink hole with the drill in reverse. You are effectively grinding the surface of the countersink flat as opposed to cutting into it. Try this first on a piece of scrap, I found the results quite impressive!

CUTTING CIRCULAR OBJECTS

When cutting any round materials like dowel, rods or PVC tubing, you can use your bench hook to hold it steady. Or, even better, clamp it to the bench to stop it rolling while you cut.

DRILLING DOWN

Always drill a hole with the timber standing up and your body over it. It is easier to drill a straight hole when you are pushing the drill downwards and you can keep check more easily using your eye by sighting down the drill bit along the length of the timber. I find that drilling vertically makes it easier to drill holes straight.

DRILLING INTO THE END GRAIN

When drilling into end grain, especially on wide-grained timber, the drill will tend to want to drift off-centre away from any dark lines in the timber (which are hard), and into the more blonde, softer timber. Try light pressure on the drill until the hole is established (perhaps try a pilot hole with a smaller drill bit), after which you can go for it. Or use a dowel jig—a device that holds a drill bit steady in a precise spot.

DRILLING INTO SMALL PIECES OF TIMBER

Small pieces of timber will tend to spin if not held firmly enough, so always use a clamp, multi grips, pliers or a bench vice when drilling lengthways.

If the timber does spin, don't try to grab the timber, just stop the drill.

DRILLING TO CONSISTENT DEPTHS

If you have several holes to drill, all at the same depth, then wrap a piece of masking tape around the drill bit at the depth required. Be sure to leave the masking tape overhanging to create a flag—as you reach the correct depth the flag will clean the surface and begin to drag on the timber making it easier to see when you have achieved the right depth.

DRILLING WITH A HOLESAW

Whenever possible, drill through one side of the timber until roughly half the cut is complete. Then flip the timber over and drill through the timber. This will be a neater cut, and also makes it easier to remove the core piece from the holesaw after drilling.

DRILLING WITH A SPEEDBOR OR SPADE BIT

Whenever possible, drill through one side of the timber just until the tip of the centre bit comes through. Then flip the timber over and, using the centre hole as a starting point, drill through the timber. This is an easier and neater way to drill the hole.

GLUED DOWEL JOINTS

When driving dowel into a hole where there is no exit hole for glue to escape, whittle a chamfer (an angled surface cut) off the dowel, similar to a flake of coconut or almond, to make a slanted end. This allows any glue in the hole to escape and make space for the dowel as you drive the dowel into position.

GLUING AND NAILING

Before adding glue, drive nails so that the tip of the nail just appears through the other side of the first piece of timber. The nail tip will act as a holding pin and help locate the pieces of timber, which will stop them sliding out of place as you drive the nails with a hammer to join the pieces together. Remember to check the positioning before you drive any nails, especially the first nail.

GLUING TO SEAL TIMBER

When possible, and especially when a join is going to be exposed to the weather, smear PVA glue over all parts of the timber that will be concealed by the join. This acts as a sealer and protects the hidden timber from moisture. Do this especially on endgrain, as that often sucks up moisture and rots first.

GLUING WITH HOT GLUE AND PVA

To glue a joint that's strong and easy to handle instantly without using screws or nails, use both PVA and hot glue.

The PVA goes on first, but don't put down one continuous line of glue—make sure you leave spaces along the glue line. Then dob spots of hot glue in the spaces. You'll have a couple of seconds to get the join in position before the hot glue binds the materials together. The hot glue gives you a temporary hold and the PVA will create the stronger hold when dry.

Keep in mind that hot glue is thick and dries quickly. Apply generous pressure while the glue is hot and runny so that the joining pieces can come together with minimal gaps.

HOUSING JOINTS

A housing joint is when one piece houses into another. It is very simple joinery and adds strength and stability to the join.

Mark the width of one piece of timber onto the other. Also mark how deep you would like the housing to be on the timber edge. Then make a cut on the waste side of each line down to your housing depth (generally this should be no more than half the thickness of the timber).

A couple more cuts between the lines into the waste timber makes chiselling out much easier and more accurate. You may wish to take a housing to half the depth of both timbers, so that pieces of the same thickness fit into each other, finishing flush.

If you have a drop saw or circular saw you can make many cuts close together at the pre-set required depth. Then hit across the checkout area with a hammer knocking away much of the waste. Then you just need to tidy up with a hammer and chisel.

Be sure to hold your work steady with clamps.

JIGSAW

CUTTING CORNERS WITH A JIGSAW

An easy method for when you come to a corner cut is to drill an 8mm hole at the corner first. This allows you to cut right to the corner and then, with the blade stopped and sitting in the pre-drilled hole, you can re-adjust your positioning and turn the blade easily within the hole to begin cutting in the other direction. Just make sure that any holes you drill are within the waste timber to avoid making a mess of the finished job.

Another method for speeding up corner cuts is to cut right to the corner. Then pull the blade backwards some distance before returning to a forward cut. Veer off the line before the corner, cutting into the waste material and turn slowly as you move the blade forward to meet up with the cutting line somewhere after the corner.

Once you have cut the majority of the job out, you can return to the corners cutting into them easily from either direction.

Whenever you are turning a jigsaw blade around a corner it is essential to make sure the blade is also moving forward. The blade can then cut as it turns. Turning a stationary blade will just twist the blade, even though it is moving up and down, burn the timber and eventually snap the blade.

For any jigsaw blade, when cutting tighter curves a vertical cutting position for the blade is best.

FAST AND FINE JIGSAW BLADES

A fast cut blade is very coarse and makes very quick, but often messy, cuts. It is usually best used with the tilt on the jigsaw leaning the blade forward (every jigsaw has settings for blade tilt).

The fine cut blade makes a far neater, but slower, cut. This blade is best for when you are cutting right to your finished line and just want a light sand afterwards. The tilt on the jigsaw should be straight up and down, unless you are cutting straighter lines—you can lean the blade forward slightly to increase the speed of the cut for these.

SCROLLING BLADE

A scrolling blade is a narrow blade that is better for cutting tighter curves. It is slower to cut though, so don't rush or the blade will start to bend off square and the cut won't look neat.

LOCATING A TIMBER FRAMING STUD

Timber studs are often part of the structural framing of a house and are the ideal fixing point in many situations. They are generally spaced either 450mm or 600mm between centres and are 35–50mm in thickness. I find a reliable way of locating studs without a stud finder is to knock gently across the wall and listen to the pitch of the knock.

First, you should apply pressure to the wall in the area you would like to find a stud (using a clean hand). This ensures that the wall sheeting is pressed against the timber stud which will increase the difference in pitch of the knock. A deep pitch indicates a hollow area, a higher pitch indicates something solid behind the face of the

wall. Check a couple of locations to confirm what you are hearing.

You should nearly always have a stud extending floor-to-ceiling either side of a window, usually in line with the architrave just outside the line of the window frame. Try knocking here first to give a good comparison of the sounds of the knocks in your desired fixing location.

Be sure that you check the location of pipes and power cables on the other side of a wall prior to drilling into the wall.

LOCKING NUTS

A locking nut is a second nut that, when tightened against a first nut, provides a locking feature which prevents either nut from working loose. The first nut does not have to be over-tightened either.

This is useful where you require a slightly loose nut to move freely. You can unlock the nut to tighten or loosen the join.

Fitting a locking nut requires the use of two spanners, or a spanner and a shifter or socket.

MARKING UP USING A FINGER GAUGE

The easiest way to mark a line along the edge of a length of timber is to use your finger! Hold the pencil in the desired position, with your finger resting against the top-edge of the timber. Then, without moving the position of the pencil or your finger, run them both along the length of wood and draw a line a consistent distance from the edge of the timber.

This is great for marking out screw positions without needing a tape measure or straight edge.

PAINTING AND DECORATING

Always remember with paint that many thin coats will look better than one thick one.

ACRYLIC PAINT

Acrylic paint dries a lot quicker than oil-based enamels, is easier to use and, some would say, more forgiving (with water clean-up), so it is often the paint of choice, especially when painting and decorating with children.

The downside is that it doesn't dry as hard as

oil paint so the finish can be quite sticky, and it is not as durable.

When using acrylics, leave your brush or roller in the tray with the paint between coats and drape a wet rag over the tray and leave it in a shady spot. You will be good to go as soon as the job is dry enough for a second coat.

OIL-BASED PAINTS

Save time and turps! When you finish with one coat, leave the paint on the roller and wrap it in cling film to keep the air off it and put it in the shade ready for use, even up to a few days later. But leave the empty tray out in the sun. I use two trays alternately between coats. The second coat gets a fresh tray and by the third, I can pour over the completely dried paint in the first tray without worrying about getting lumps.

Be sure not to put too much paint on each coat of colour when using oil-based paint. Thick coats will usually get runs.

PAINT TRAYS

It is best if you can only pour into the tray the paint you need for each coat. Then you don't have to pour paint back into the paint tin, which can contaminate the paint.

PRIMER

This doesn't need to be a complete cover of paint, keep it thin. It will dry in minutes and is simply a bonding agent for your finished colour.

Under very bright and deep-coloured paints, especially reds, grey is a great tint to add to your primer/undercoat. The top, finished colour seems to achieve a far better finish in fewer coats. Sometimes one coat of colour over a grey undercoat can be enough.

PILOT HOLES

Pilot holes will help the keep nails or screws driving into the desired location and prevent splitting. A pilot hole should be smaller than the nail or screw, so it still allows them to grip. As a rule of thumb for nails, I drill pilot holes at two-thirds the thickness of the nail.

When selecting the drill bit for a pilot hole for screws you should line the screw up behind the shaft of the drill bit—the perfect pilot hole bit should allow you to easily see the thread of the screw only.

Pilot holes are important because it is the thread of the screw that cuts into the timber and has all the holding power. The solid metal part in the middle just creates sideways pressure as it is forced into the timber which can split the job.

PLYWOOD

To minimise warping, undercoat large pieces of plywood as soon as possible, and never leave out in the sun.

SANDING CORNERS AND EDGES SMOOTH

It's good to round off any sharp corners from timber that will later be handled or played with by kids. So before sanding with a palm sander, rub the corners of timber gently on some driveway concrete first. It will remove the sharpness so you can then palm-sand smooth without tearing the sandpaper. (It's a slightly primitive method, but still effective!)

SANDPAPER

You'll need a variety of grits to get the perfect finish on your projects. The lower the number, the coarser the sandpaper:

40-80 grit Use this grade sandpaper for rounding corners and edges, and for a first sanding of some recycled materials.

120 grit This mid-grade sandpaper will result in a smoother finish. It is ideal for preparation before painting.

180 grit Use this fine-grade sandpaper to sand out more coarse sanding lines and achieve an extremely smooth surface suitable for oils and clear coatings.

SCREWS–POSITIONING

Put the first screw at a distance at least the length of the screw you are using in from the end of the timber to ensure the screws coming in from different sides don't hit each other. Plus, keeping a minimum distance from the end of the timber you are screwing into means that it is less likely to split.